MY LIFE WITH BIRDS

The Education and Successes of a Wildlife Artist

Hooded Mergansers
1986
oil on canvas board
6" x 19 ³⁄₈"
Collection of the artist

These ducks are found primarily in woods and lake country and are known as "fish" ducks. They have a slender tapering bill edged with sharp tooth-like edges for catching fish. Good swimmers and divers, they often pursue prey underwater.

MY LIFE WITH BIRDS

The Education and Successes of a Wildlife Artist

Angus Shortt

CAVENDISH INVESTING LTD.

A Richard Bonnycastle Book V

Text researched and compiled by Heather Robertson
Visuals coordinated by Gary Essar
Designed by Bill Stewart
Edited for this edition by Jennifer Glossop
Copy edited by Shaun Oakey

Photo Credits
All color photography by Ernest Mayer, Winnipeg except
    Tye Gregg, Winnipeg – back cover
    Terry Sweeney, Memphis – pages 87 and 88
    Meier Camera, Midland, Wisconsin – pages 62, 63 and 89

National Library of Canada Cataloguing in Publication

Shortt, Angus, 1908-
        My life with birds : the education and successes of a wildlife
artist / Angus Shortt.

Includes index.
ISBN 0-919664-10-5

        1. Shortt, Angus, 1908- 2. Wildlife artists--Canada--Biography.
3. Ornithologists--Manitoba--Biography. I. Title.

QH31.S53A3 2003   759.11   C2003-904352-5

Printed and bound in Canada by Friesens

The publisher has donated the total costs and proceeds from this book to the Freshwater Initiative of the Institute for Wetland and Waterfowl Research, the research arm of Ducks Unlimited Canada.

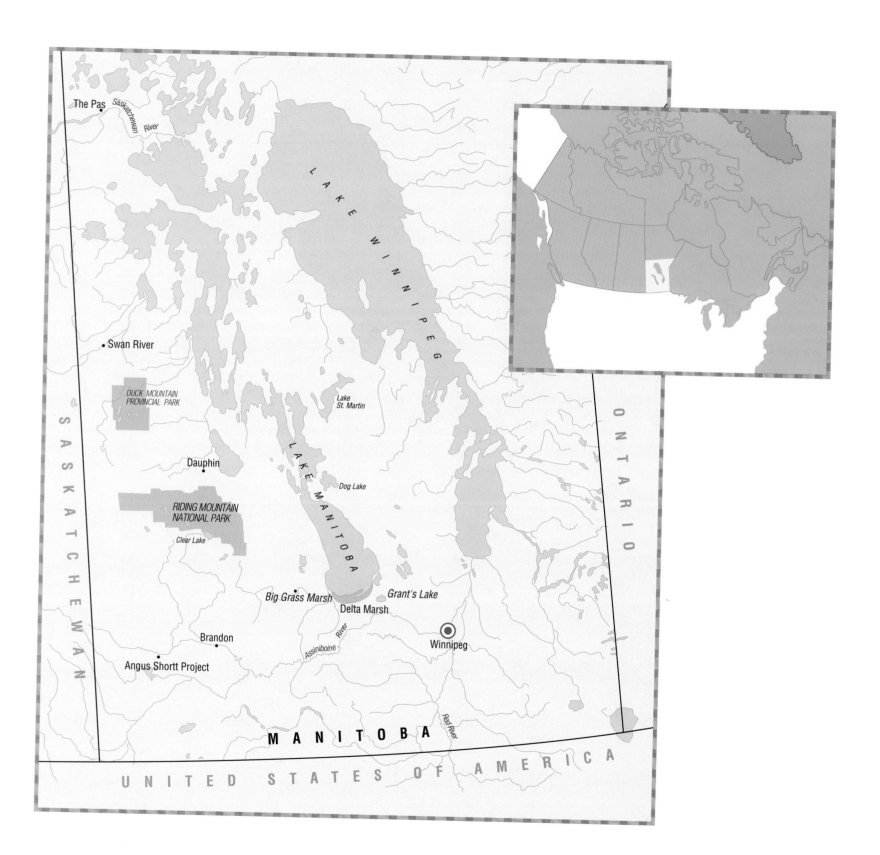

Table of Contents

Chapter One: **Early Years** 11

Chapter Two: **Work at Brigden's** 15

Chapter Three: **A Fascination with Birds** 19

Chapter Four: **Out of Work** 25

Chapter Five: **Museum Work** 35

Chapter Six: **The Study of Birds** 43

Chapter Seven: **Ducks Unlimited** 53

Chapter Eight: **An Artistic Career** 65

Afterword: Ducks Unlimited's Freshwater Initiative 84

Biographical Notes 86

Illustration Identification 93

Index 94

Canvasbacks, Delta, Manitoba

1959
oil on canvas board
21 ¹⁵/₁₆" x 30 ³/₁₆"
Collection of Richard Bonnycastle, Calgary

In the spring, marsh water is clear and reflects the color of the sky. In this painting, the reeds hadn't greened up yet from the year before.

CHAPTER ONE

Early Years

I was born in Belfast, Ireland, on September 25, 1908. My mother, Emma McMeekin Shortt, was an accomplished artist, having taken lessons in both watercolor and oil painting. My father, Henry Shortt, had no artistic leanings whatsoever, but shared a love of horses and dogs with his brother Michael.

Father was owner and proprietor of a public house known as the Beehive, on the Lisburn Road, the main thoroughfare in Belfast. The Beehive was a gathering spot for all sorts of characters, from horse fanciers to dog lovers to just plain imbibers. Father knew well the seamy side of the booze business and the hazards of the July twelfth Orangemen's Parade, when opposing factions let go with bricks and whatever came to hand. Almost annually he had to replace windows and stock smashed in such outbursts. Little wonder, then, that he made up his mind to get out of Belfast.

In 1911 my parents and I came to Canada and settled in Winnipeg, Manitoba, where my brother Terry was born later that year. Winnipeg was then a booming, hustling frontier city of 150,000 people. With its elegant yellow-brick Grain Exchange, monumental bank buildings, five-story warehouses and an Eaton's department store that occupied an entire city block, Winnipeg could rightly boast of being the "Gateway to the West" and the "Chicago of the North." As a railway hub, the city's wealth came from trade. To many of the thousands of immigrants who daily poured off the trains, good jobs in Winnipeg were as attractive as free land to the west.

Father took a job as a conductor on the Winnipeg Street Railway, a position he held for forty years until his retirement. My mother went to

Sharp-tailed grouse dancing

AHS.
1930
Deer Lodge

Sharp-tailed Grouse Dancing
1930
graphite on paper
5 ¾" x 6 ⅜"
Collection of the artist

I did this early pencil sketch when I was still living in my parents' home. These birds were common in the woods close by.

work at Eaton's in the artists' materials department. This was a pleasant time for her, during which she became acquainted with many of the city's top artists.

In 1916 we moved near the Minto Armoury. The First World War was at its height, and Terry and I were fascinated with the parades of regiments up and down the street. But Father wanted to have a dog again, and since automobile traffic was increasing, he would have had to walk the dog on a leash. So it was that in 1918 we moved again, this time completely out of the city to a house in Deer Lodge that we bought for $2,700. Guildford Street, on the western outskirts of the city, was near the terminus of the Winnipeg Street Railway's Portage Avenue line. To the south, a footbridge over the Assiniboine River led to Assiniboine Park; nearby, the Deer Lodge convalescent home for wounded war veterans occupied the property that had given the area its name.

Near our comfortable two-story home lay the eight-hundred-acre Strathcona Estate, a prairie wilderness of aspen woods and scrub oak bluffs, marshes, native grasslands and wildflowers, pasture and farmland that stretched north of the Assiniboine River and included part of what is now the Winnipeg International Airport. The deserted and overgrown estate was an exciting place for two adventurous, inquisitive young boys to explore, and it was here that Terry and I learned to delight in nature and to indulge our curiosity about birds.

It was also at this time that Terry and I began to show an interest in drawing. Mother encouraged us, and often obtained sample art instruction books for us from Eaton's. Generally, these dealt with flower designs for her hobby, painting on china, but she also brought home some illustrated nature books. These came from England, and their subject matter was English or European with some articles dealing with the wildlife of Africa. I began to copy pictures of birds, flowers and animals and to dabble in watercolors and pastels.

A few years later — I believe I was in grade six — I painted a number of woodpeckers on a single sheet of paper, all copied from illustrations in nature books. Few of the birds were native to Manitoba, let alone Canada, but my teacher was delighted and tacked the paper up on the wall for all to see. In 1922, I copied in watercolor a series of twenty-four birds from the back of a Hudson's Bay Company calendar. This time, there were four Manitoba species.

Mother eventually stopped working at Eaton's. Instead, once a week she gave lessons in china painting. As Christmas approached, she always had many orders for china sets, vases and a variety of decorative pieces. I helped her to some extent, painting the fine black outlines in preparation for the china's first firing.

In 1923, I found a cluster of bittersweet twined around an old poplar tree in the woods. The yellow casings had opened and spread out, like four petals, to expose the bright orange berries. I climbed up and collected a bunch. Mother arranged it in a dark blue vase, which she placed on the floor beside the fireplace. For the annual student art show at Linwood School, where Terry and I were students, I designed a 8" x 11" panel, with the bittersweet painted on a light gray background, the vine in an upward curve to the top where the uppermost tendrils arched together, the orange and yellow showing up in contrast with the gray ground color. I won first prize, which, I believe, was one dollar.

I also began painting the chickadees and blue jays that flocked around our bird feeders in the winter months. The chickadees became bold enough to take seeds from my hand, giving me a good close-up look at these sprightly little birds. In 1926, after Terry and I were given snowshoes for Christmas, we were able to tramp through the woods and fields of the Strathcona Estate as happily in winter as in summer.

Edge of the Poplar Bluff
1930
watercolor and graphite on paper board
8" x 11"
Collection of the artist

*I often walked near our house to view
the sunset in winter. I tried to paint
the effect of the sun on the trees.*

CHAPTER TWO

Working at Brigden's

Once I turned seventeen, I was expected to find work. My goal was to become a commercial artist. Accompanied by my father, I went to Brigden's, then the leading art firm in western Canada. I received an immediate interview and a job. But since there was no vacancy in the commercial art department, I was signed on to a five-year apprenticeship as a wood engraver. Starting pay was six dollars for a forty-four-hour week.

The work was close and exacting. It involved preparing illustrations for the Eaton's catalogs, which were then printed in black and white only. Eaton's, a national department-store and mail-order chain similar to Sears in the United States, sold everything from jewelry and chinaware to hardware, lace curtains and even large farm implements.

The work tended to fluctuate with the season. Eaton's produced spring, fall and winter catalogs, and each required at least three months of constant work, with much overtime and tight deadlines. At such times, the engravers often worked straight through until ten or eleven at night. One of my jobs as apprentice was to go out to get coffee or tea and sandwiches for them. In between catalogs, hours were regular — eight to five — and I got in a lot of practice engraving and drawing.

From 1928 to 1929, Brigden's sent me to the Winnipeg School of Art. Here I learned to sketch, in charcoal and, to some extent, in watercolor, plaster casts of heads and figures. The instructor was L. LeMoine FitzGerald, the school's principal and a nationally recognized artist. He was to join Canada's Group of Seven in 1932, the last artist to do so.

FitzGerald was a quiet man who, in his teaching, emphasized the contours characteristic of his own work. He'd shine a light on a statue at an angle to create a shadow that brought out the outline. We drew that in charcoal. FitzGerald's soft, abstract style was antithetical to the hard, precise lines required of a wood engraver and was considered far too "modernist" by my employers at Brigden's.

Eventually, I was allowed to begin work as an apprentice engraver. For wood engraving, we used blocks of wood that came either as solid boxwood or as a base of maple with a one-eighth-inch boxwood veneer. Boxwood has an extremely tight grain, ideal for cutting with engraving tools for it will not burr or fray no matter in what direction it is tooled. Articles to be engraved were either drawn on a specially prepared white surface or printed on it by a photographic method.

My engraving tools, which I still have, cost me twenty-four dollars, or four weeks' wages, in my first year. They came in a set of twenty-four with different points, rounded, square-ended and graded to various widths and similar to those used by gold- and silversmiths. There were also tools that had two to six points so that, with a single cut, several white lines could be engraved at once. A broad-ended tool, like a small chisel, was used to cut a wide outline around the engraving so that, when printed, the engraving could be easily cut out with scissors for mounting on the page layouts. Cutting out the engravings was one of my first jobs.

In 1929, three years into my apprenticeship, I was taught the intricacies of photoprinting, by which the negatives of product images were printed onto the engravers' boxwood blocks. It was a promotion, but I had to work alone in an eight-by-ten-foot darkroom at the end of the long hall that separated Brigden's commercial art department from its wood engraving department. To keep in touch with daily events, I peeked though holes in the beaverboard walls of the darkroom and watched the comings and goings in the hall.

There was plenty to watch. Brigden's, like every commercial art establishment, employed its share of free spirits, alcoholics and eccentrics. The head photographer, Joseph Hall, a slightly built man of medium height, wore an immaculately trimmed beard and mustache in the style of King George V and arrived for work sporting a black three-quarter-length frock coat with a black velvet collar, a black derby and gloves to match. Hall, like the other supervisors, went home every afternoon at precisely five, but many of the artists and engravers, including me, worked nights to remain caught up with our assignments. At midnight, my darkroom, far from being a dull spot, was a hub of clandestine conviviality.

I should explain how this came about. Drinking was, of course, prohibited during working hours. But after hours, with no boss to oversee them, the commercial artists felt an urge to let off steam. It so happened that my darkroom window overlooked a lane alongside the building, and this arrangement gave my colleagues the idea of using it to get beer into the building without risking detection on the main or freight elevators. I was assured that I would in no way be held responsible if they were caught. I must say, I was ready for a bit of adventure too, and I could see no reason to stand in their way.

One of the men would drive his car to the lane after dark with the beer and park beneath the window. Another would be in my darkroom with a coil of rope. The rope would be lowered, a case of beer secured and

Blue Jay
1930
wood engraving
3 ³/₁₆″ x 4 ³/₈″
Collection of the artist

Once I became more proficient with the wood-engraving technique, I created a few of subjects I was more interested in.

hoisted up. Needless to say, this arrangement made me very popular with the art department.

In spite of the shenanigans, I found much of my apprenticeship tedious and frustrating. I had to make countless proofs of others' engravings, and practice engraving letters of the alphabet in intricate Gothic lettering. Another exercise involved designing and painting elaborate borders, using opaque white paint on black, dark green or brown cards, making sure that both sides of the border were identical. These exercises occupied my time during the slack season. In the summer, I had four weeks' vacation, two without pay. By the end of my apprenticeship in 1931, I was earning twenty-five dollars a week.

Mallard Pair
1928
watercolor on board
6 ¹/₂" x 9 ¹/₈"
Collection of the artist

My very first painting of mallards,
painted on July 17, 1928.

CHAPTER THREE

A Fascination with Birds

Since 1927, my interest in birds had been stimulated by Bert Cartwright, a neighbor and a passionate amateur naturalist who did much of his birding on the Strathcona Estate. Cartwright, well known for his bird column, "Wild Wings," in the *Winnipeg Tribune*, corresponded regularly with Percy A. Taverner, Dominion ornithologist at the National Museum of Canada, in Ottawa, and author of the definitive reference book *Birds of Western Canada*.

In 1928 Cartwright had persuaded Terry and me to send a selection of our bird paintings to Taverner for his appraisal. In an accompanying letter dated October 19, 1928, Cartwright wrote: "Two young artists who have been taking a great deal of interest in nature generally came under my notice last fall and I set them to work painting birds. They have done nothing along this line prior to this year so you will be looking at their first efforts. They show in my opinion such originality and general merit that I suggested they send them down to you on the chance that you may be able to use some of them in your forthcoming book, *The Birds of Canada*. If you could, it would be a great encouragement to them. You will of course be able to pick out some flaws here and there but the astonishing part of the whole business is the wholesome originality of their work. They are bringing a new note into bird portraiture and if the improvement they have shown so far is maintained, I venture to say they will soon be in the front rank. What is your opinion?

"The boys themselves are very quiet and retiring sorts of fellows.

They are very observant and grasp things very quickly. They have none of the so-called artistic temperament, listen quietly to criticism and then when a picture is repainted, as one or two of them have been, you find every little detail of your criticism has been faithfully taken care of. There is not a spark of jealousy between them."

Taverner, himself accomplished at drawing birds, replied: "I thank you exceedingly for giving me the opportunity of seeing the pictures. They are by far the most promising beginnings for a bird artist that I have seen in a long time. They are so good in fact and your reports of the painters are so encouraging that I feel they demand a real and a serious review. I can see a brilliant future for either of these boys as bird artists should they decide to progress in that direction and will continue to improve and study. I have seen several good starts that have failed to arrive usually through cessation of serious effort and too great a satisfaction of achievement.

"These pictures do show a new viewpoint and are very refreshing. They also show a good command of technique and that the boys can put on a clean wash of great brilliance which is a notable accomplishment in itself. They also have a certain touch and in the landscape there is little fumbling. I imagine much of this is due to wood-cut experience where certainty of touch is essential. Those sunset skies are charming but I should like to warn against the possibility of their becoming a formula. Good in themselves, but likely to become mechanical.

"The things the boys know they know very well and do well, but they have considerable to learn. The birds themselves show this strongly. They know little of feather tracts. Feather system is entirely lacking except in the wing of the water thrush, that I should judge is drawn from a real wing. You cannot draw birds unless you have an intimate knowledge of feather tracts and feather groups. You have to know them better than any systematic ornithologist. Of course you do not show these tracts as a rule in their theoretic detail, but unless you do indicate them, and indicate them correctly, you fail to get the characteristic birdy feel. Art may be a process of elimination, but unless you know what should go in you cannot leave it out. Leaving out non-essentials and missing what you do not know are two very different things. Every feather need not be drawn, but every one that is indicated should show its proper character.

"I should advise a strict and systematic drawing from nature, not so much at present to make pictures, but to place down just what they see, and to learn to see what is before them. Drawing from living birds, chickens, tame ducks, will help a lot in bird fundamentals. Captive hawks and owls, even canaries are good. Dead birds are also useful to show how feathers lay and mass. Making carefully detailed studies of wings, bills and feet are excellent practice in gaining a knowledge of their construction. Also the accessories, branches, leaves and trees. The unfortunate thing is that bird men have to do so much without models, drawing from memory, and this is only possible after long familiarity with the subject. Most people think that branches and clouds, for instance, can be almost anything. One has to be saturated with the feel of these things before he can evolve them out of his inner consciousness.

"As for using any of these pictures in the bird book, I do not think it would be best for either the

Snowy Owl Near Rosser, Man

A.Shortt.
1929

Snowy Owl Near Rosser, Manitoba
1929
graphite and watercolor on paper
5 ³/₈" x 7 ⁵/₈"
Collection of the artist

I had an early interest in how birds fly. Owls soar
silently in search of food. I completed this watercolor
from field observations and pencil sketches.

book or the artists to do so. They are better now than some of the old ones used, but we hope for still better things from these boys who are too good to go off at half cock. All the youthful geniuses are apt to get too much thoughtless praise from the ill informed.

"I hope neither you nor they will take all this amiss. If I thought less of them I would say much less. They have great promise, but it is still only promise and needs a lot more study and hard work."

I created this design for a Ducks Unlimited Christmas card in the 1950s. The original drawing is now in the collection of Mr. and Mrs. Bill Leitch, Winnipeg.

When he returned our paintings, Taverner went on to stress the limitations of bird art: "Leading bird artists today are ornithologists first and artists afterwards. If the rewards seem sufficient to you boys, and you are willing and anxious to work hard for it, I should say — Go to it. I think you have the artistic ability for development; if you have the same interest in aesthetic and *scientific* bird study success looks very promising. But don't waste time on it unless really in earnest. It's no use turning a good commercial designer into a second-rate bird illustrator — we have enough of them now. I consider your work to be good enough to be frank about it. If I can be of any assistance at any time I will be glad to offer it."

Taking Taverner's advice to heart, Terry and I knuckled down to draw from life and to sketch birds' heads, beaks, eyes, feet and wings from specimens in Cartwright's collection. Although I was still working long hours at Brigden's and had little time to spare for bird study, Terry and I sent a selection of new paintings to Taverner in January 1929. Noticing "considerable improvement," Taverner offered to buy two pictures, a blue jay and a Canada jay, for ten dollars each. But Taverner was critical of both the birds' anatomy and their backgrounds — the blue jay had to be repainted to remove an offending branch — and he made it clear the Shortt boys would have a hard time challenging his favorite bird painters, Allan Brooks in British Columbia and Louis Agassiz Fuertes, the most admired American bird artist since John James Audubon. "The difficulties against commercial success are much greater now than they were with either Brooks or Fuertes," Taverner warned. "They began when there was practically a clear field and no one who could seriously compete with them. Today your work is naturally contrasted with theirs, and a rather large number of others who are much in your condition, and some further advanced and already more in the public eye. I am afraid that I do not know how to help you in this direction." To Cartwright, Taverner wrote about the "strong competition" that Terry and I were facing: "We have numbers of pretty good bird artists now and the standards are correspondingly high but not insurmountable."

Taverner's advice may have been overly pessimistic. Most bird art was, as he had implied, mediocre, and public taste was changing. Fuertes, who had been killed in a car accident in 1927, was criticized for weak backgrounds and a flat, two-dimensional style; Allan Brooks, whose paintings Taverner had featured in *Birds of Western Canada*, was considered by some to be more a decorative illustrator than an artist. Terry's and my strongest competition came from two American artists who were still virtually unknown: Francis Lee Jaques at the American Museum of Natural History, in New York City, and Roger Tory Peterson, a New England painter who was only a few years older than me and whose *Peterson Field Guides* continue to be famous today.

However, unlike the Americans, Taverner had no museum budget to buy or commission art, and Ottawa had no wealthy patrons willing to pay for it. Taverner generously gave me names and addresses of museums and publications that might be interested in buying my work, but nothing came of it.

By 1931, I was becoming very discouraged. Terry, on the other hand, who had also studied with LeMoine FitzGerald at the Winnipeg School of Art, had shown such precocious promise as an artist and collector of bird specimens that he was hired by the Royal Ontario Museum, in Toronto, in 1930. Terry worked at the museum for forty-four years and produced meticulously drawn illustrations for their many publications and dioramas.

Harlequin Ducks
1964
watercolor on paper
8 $^{1}/_{16}$" x 11 $^{1}/_{16}$"
Collection of the artist

These ducks are rare in Manitoba and have been sighted around Hudson Bay. Their usual habitat is the west coast, and they are sometimes seen on the east coast. They get their name from their bright, clown-like plumage.

CHAPTER FOUR

Out of Work

The second year of the Great Depression was an inauspicious time for any young man starting to make his way in the world, and Winnipeg, with an economy now almost totally dependent on agriculture, had been hard hit by the collapse in the price of wheat. For me, the rumblings of a business recession were ominous.

Late in 1931, I was informed that my job was terminated, since Eaton's had cut back heavily on new engravings. Five years' work were wiped out just when I was getting a decent wage. Things got worse. In 1932 the entire wood engraving department was closed down, and much of the commercial art work was transferred to Toronto. Despite a letter of recommendation, I was unable to obtain employment with any of the other engraving firms in the city and came away rather despondent.

Fortunately, I was still living at home, and my parents encouraged me to put my unexpected free time to good use. Father encouraged me to continue with nature study, with birds a priority. To help, he bought me a second-hand pair of Zeiss binoculars. Though they had a limited field of vision and individual eye focusing, they nevertheless served me well.

In 1932, when museum collections of bird specimens were, at best, patchy, a museum or private collector would pay fifty cents to a dollar for a well-prepared skin. Manitoba, with its diverse marsh, upland and woodland habitat, was scientifically significant, and specimens of

Manitoba birds were in demand. I applied for and received a federal collecting permit, issued solely for the collecting of birds for scientific purposes. Thus armed with my binoculars and a shotgun, I embarked on a serious study of birds.

I had almost memorized Taverner's *Birds of Western Canada* and had studied *Birds of New York State*, a folio of color plates by Fuertes, but I had insufficient first-hand knowledge of birds, and my paintings were amateurish at best. One ambitious effort, done in 1928, was a watercolor of a pair of mallards sitting on the water (see page 18). I kept it, and I am glad now that I did, as it shows the struggle to portray a subject about which I knew so little but was to learn so much in the years to come.

I found sketching and painting birds difficult. My rigid training as an engraver had instilled in me a desire for sharp, clean outlines and minute detail. As a result, my bird drawings tended to be hard and stiff. My watercolors were also too hard in outline and showed too much fine detail. It took me many years to loosen up my technique and acquire a freer style. I tore up many partly finished paintings in disgust.

Soon, however, I began to look about with a more educated eye for clues that various habitats gave about the birds. My interest in the Strathcona Estate, known by then as the Silver Heights farm, became intense. Along the Assiniboine River, gravel and mud bars were exposed at low water, attracting transient shorebirds, gulls, herons and the occasional bittern, while the river itself played host to migrating waterfowl. The high, steep clay banks afforded nesting sites for a colony of rough-winged and bank swallows and, at times, a pair of kingfishers. Bur oaks, with an undergrowth of hazel, willow, chokecherry, saskatoon and hawthorn, grew to the edge of the riverbank and con-

tinued north of Portage Avenue. These oak woods, with many fine old trees, occupied a large portion of the south end of the farm. Birds associated with the oaks included kingbirds, wood pewees and a surprising number of cedar waxwings. Ruby-throated hummingbirds, too, built their quaint little nests on the gnarled and lichen-covered branches of the oaks, using the lichen to decorate their nests. The nests, held together with spiderwebs, were amazingly camouflaged. Other occasional residents were Cooper's and broad-winged hawks.

Halfway up the farm, poplar woods predominated. The lower areas, inundated each spring with several inches of water, were home to great choruses of frogs that trilled in magnificent volume, especially at night. Several pairs of ruffed grouse nested in the poplar woods. The northern half of the farm had formerly been sown to crops, but, with disuse, had reverted to short grass. On the west side of this open grassland was a small, willow-bordered marsh beside two groves of oaks. This little marsh harbored a small colony of red-winged blackbirds, usually one or two pairs of sora rails, a short-billed marsh wren and a yellow-throated warbler. One or two pairs of crows regularly nested in the oaks. A pair of horned owls and a pair of broad-winged hawks each nested on one occasion on the dry, sun-baked grassland. Kildeers, meadowlarks, horned larks and savannah sparrows were yearly nesters, as well as, on occasion, chestnut-collared longspurs, Sprague's pipit and bobolink.

Traversing the length of the farm on its east side was a deep ditch that ran parallel to a railway embankment, a long-abandoned spur line connecting with the CPR line along Saskatchewan Avenue. The rails had been torn up and only a few of the old log ties remained. Willows grew profusely on each side of the

WESTERN MEADOWLARK
ADULT AND YOUNG.

Angus H. Shortt.
1932.

Western Meadowlark: Adult and Young
1932
watercolor on board
14 $^{15}/_{16}$" x 10 $^{1}/_{16}$"
Collection of the artist

I exhibited this watercolor at the American Ornithologists' Union meeting in St. Louis, Missouri, in 1932. It shows my early interest in putting in a lot of detail, something I learned from my wood-engraving experience. The plants, which are native to Manitoba, are another of my interests.

ditch, which held water most of the year, along almost its entire length. Spring and fall, this ditch formed a natural "highway" for hordes of migrating sparrows, warblers and blackbirds.

I kept my eyes on the ground, too, noting the wildflowers that carpeted various areas at different times of the year: prairie crocus, hoary puccoon, wood violet and trillium in spring, succeeded in summer and fall by yellow lady's slipper, wild rose, prairie lily, wild bergamot, wild sunflower, blazing stars, gentians, asters and goldenrod. I recorded ninety species of plants and wildflowers (including poison ivy) over eight years.

For an aspiring artist, a serious study of birds meant more than making lists of bird sightings, and I began observing birds' behavior. In my field notes for November 26, 1932, I wrote: "Richardson's [boreal] owl feeding on a house sparrow near the house. The sparrow was held firmly with the claws and the owl tore off chunks of the flesh and feathers with its bill, which were swallowed whole, feathers and all. A flock of about 30 sparrows were perched around it in the oak trees. Although keeping a respectful distance, they 'chirped' continuously in loud protest, but the owl merely glared at them between bites."

Every day, if possible, I went out into the field. I wandered about the fields, woods and marshes, notebook and sketchpad in hand, studying birds in their natural surroundings. I liked spring and fall the best, for then each day brought some new experience and thrill. In winter, I was out almost daily, snowshoeing across the drifts and along well-known woodland trails, intent on glimpses of sharp-tailed grouse, ruffed grouse, chickadees and blue jays. There was always added surprise in the appearance of such winter visitors as bohemian waxwings and grosbeaks.

I posed for this photo on a mild day in late 1932, before heading out on a snowshoe tramp over the nearby Silver Heights farm. Our house on Guildford Street, seen in the background, was then on the outskirts of Winnipeg with no buildings to the north or across the street.

On one of my walks around Deer Lodge, near our Guildford Street home, I discovered this sleeping boreal owl. It had just eaten a mouse and was so content that I was able to walk right up to it and take the first picture. Then I kicked the tree to wake it up for the second.

One morning I headed out with my camera to take some photographs of snow-laden shrubs and curving drifts. This time, I went along the east side of Silver Heights Farm, where the old railway embankment was thickly overgrown with willows and shrubs, with poplars clustered around. I had gone but a short distance when, glancing up, I saw a small owl sitting on a branch over the trail. Looking carefully, I discovered that it was a boreal owl and it was fast asleep. This species and the saw-whet owl are rare in the southern parts of the province but can be expected in the winter. They are also the smallest owls found in Manitoba, measuring about nine inches in length. Standing where I was, I wondered if I had a chance for a picture. However, the owl was perched at least a foot higher than my head, and my camera was one of those folding Kodaks with a look-down viewfinder. The only thing to do was to try to hold the camera above my head, upside down, and focus on the owl. Carefully I maneuvered into position, hoisted the camera up, got the bird in the viewfinder and snapped the shutter. The owl never moved, just partly opened its eyes, then went off to sleep again. I wanted to get a snap of it with its eyes open if possible, so I tried making noise by shuffling my snowshoes. I could not keep this up and hold my camera steady, so I tried shouting. This caused the owl to open its eyes, but only momentarily, before dozing off again. Fortunately, it showed no inclination to fly. As a last resort, I moved up as close as I dared so I could kick the trunk of the tree with the tip of my snowshoe. Unbelievably, I kicked twice with no reaction beyond a quick look before the eyes closed again. At the third kick, the owl turned sideways on the branch, its eyes open now and looking very annoyed! I quickly snapped a picture and the owl flew silently away.

I had another adventure with an owl the following year. It was a bright, sunny morning in late March, and I set out with my Irish setter, Causey, a constant companion on all my jaunts. I traversed the open prairie, where the snow was firmly packed, keeping a lookout for horned larks, which I had seen in the area a few days earlier. I scanned the open fields to the north with my binoculars, seeing nothing but the setter ranging some distance ahead.

As I watched, she paused at a small drift of snow and stood for some moments, as if attracted by something. I thought a field mouse, perhaps, but looking again I made out a rounded white form, much mottled with dark. I decided to investigate. To my surprise, the object proved to be a dead snowy owl, lying on its side by the mound of snow. Examination showed no indication of injury, and the bird was in excellent plumage, the white feathers heavily barred and spotted with dark brown. I found, however, that I could not remove it. It was frozen fast to the ground, and any attempt to pull it free would have torn away much of the breast feathering. It was such a fine specimen for me to sketch and paint that I returned home to get an ax to chop it out with. I retrieved the owl and headed home. I must have presented quite a picture, ax over one shoulder, the big owl tucked under one arm and the setter running alongside!

Thawed and cleaned, the owl proved to be a fine specimen. The only sign of injury was a small hole behind the left shoulder, possibly made by a .22 rifle bullet. The bullet might have grazed the base of the skull, damaging the brain and ultimately causing death. I made sketches of the head and wings, then photographed it before making it into a study skin.

In order to build my collection of scientific study skins, I had to learn taxidermy. I turned to Horace Hatton, a Winnipeg taxidermist whose hole-in-the-wall shop near the corner of Portage and Main was cluttered with the remains of birds, fish and animals in various stages of preparation.

Hatton taught me how skin a bird: Cut straight down the breast, then turn the skin on the head inside out and extract the bird's brain from the skull. Leave the skull, but remove the bird's body, leaving only the lower legs and wings. Dust the inside of the skin with arsenic to prevent insect infestation, pack the cavity with spongelike stuffing and sew up the incision.

On a study skin, the bird's feet are tied together and its wings closed, but Hatton, who did most of his work for sportsmen, taught me to mount birds as well. He showed me how to put a wire through the body and up into the head, then twist it around until you get the shape you want. The legs are difficult, because they have to support the weight of the bird. You put a wire down the leg, through the foot and into a block of wood, then clinch it so the bird is standing. For birds in flight, you brace the wings with wire and fan the tail. The legs are tucked up.

While skinning birds, I was able to examine the delicate colors and shapes of their feathers, as well as the individual bones and muscles of the tiny corpses that remained. I noticed, for instance, where the bird's leg met the body. On a marsh bird, it would be farther back, and on a grebe, farther back still, so that it could hardly walk on land.

By March 1932, I was confident enough in my ability to send Percy Taverner three unusual red-tailed hawk skins, with my own tentative identifications. In the parcel, I also included my latest watercolor drawings.

Taverner replied: "I see that you are getting your detail and the lay of the feathers. All that you require is facility that comes with practice to give certainty and strength. Should advise you to try to represent birds from various and unusual points of view. It is comparatively easy to draw a bird in sharp profile, but ability to foreshorten is more difficult. Should also suggest your backgrounds are a bit Christmas cardy. The sparrow hawk is not as good as the others, it is a little bit hard and fussy. The shadow on the breast is mighty good, in fact you are beginning to handle your washes very well indeed. I see also that you are learning to draw feet. You will improve on them, but you are on the right track."

From Taverner, this was high praise, but my taxidermy skills were taking precedence over my painting. The taxidermy paid off with several jobs in the hunting season, when mounted specimens were greatly in vogue with sportsmen. My first two jobs were a long-eared owl, then not protected by law, and a pair of gray partridges. I received four dollars apiece for these jobs. As well, I undertook to skin out ducks and geese for hunters, on the understanding that I could keep the skins to increase my knowledge of waterfowl. I got a quite good response to this, largely through Father's acquaintances with hunters, some of whom he met regularly on the streetcars. Of course, I had to go to their homes to skin the birds, in either the basement or the garage, but when you know how to do these things, it doesn't matter where you are. All I took along were my scalpel, scissors, a pound or two of fine sawdust and a small bag to carry the skins home in.

During hunting season, I received two unexpected additions to my collection. The first was a whistling swan. A chum of mine phoned one night to report that a friend of his had been out goose hunting and had shot the swan by mistake. He was now uncertain about how to get rid of it. Had I any use for it? I certainly did, and in less than half an hour my friend was at the door, lugging the swan in a sack. This big bird weighed sixteen to eighteen pounds, so I imagine

he had his hands full carrying it on and off the streetcar! It was the largest bird I had ever skinned — the neck seemed endless.

The second bird was a cormorant. My druggist friend, Reg Whitman, phoned after returning from a duck-hunting trip to tell me he had bagged a bird he could not identify. Could I come to see it? The drugstore was only two blocks away and I found Reg waiting for me, the cormorant lying on an old table in the back of the store. Reg took it to be a fish duck, a merganser. I said no, it was worse, it was a crow duck, and I pointed out to him the sharp, hooked beak and gular pouch. He said he had cooking it in mind. I strongly advised against this, saying it would take hours and the bird would taste like a tough old fish. I said I would skin it out for him if I could have the skin and he could try cooking it if he wished. "Take the damn thing!" he said, laughing, and got me a big brown paper bag.

I also persevered with my painting, and although sales were minimal, I did get some two- and three-dollar commissions for Christmas card designs. I specialized in 6" x 8" studies of single birds, generally chickadees, blue jays, ruby-throated hummingbirds and Baltimore orioles.

I took samples of my work to the Richardson Brothers' art store on Main Street. They were the top picture dealers in town, but times were tough. Although I made no sales, they did offer to accept my paintings in exchange for an equal value of paints, brushes or paper. Through the Natural History Society of Manitoba and a growing number of friends, I began to sell 8" x 10" pictures, with two birds and some background, for five dollars each. I did fairly well, and I was able to help a little with the groceries and purchase better artist's materials.

Head and Foot of Osprey (Adult Male)
1933
watercolor on paper
9 ¾" x 7 ¹/₁₆"
Collection of the artist

This is one of many field studies I made. I had to start painting immediately after collecting the specimen because the colors would change quickly.

It was Bert Cartwright who persuaded me to undertake a year-long scientific study of a single Manitoba bird species. At this time, it was customary for reputable ornithologists to be self-taught scholars who learned by reading, observing and comparing records — Taverner himself had achieved professional status without a university degree. Casting about for a subject, I chose a bird that was literally at my feet, a bird so small, common and colorless it had been ignored: the clay-colored sparrow. The sparrows were easy to find; colonies of them nested in the grass or in the snowberry, hawthorn and red osier dogwood bushes that covered much of the prairie in the Deer Lodge area.

Beginning when the first male sparrows arrived on May 6, 1932, I methodically observed their habitat, courtship and mating behavior, nest building (a typical nest, dismantled, contained 147 feet of grass and 43 feet of horsehair), egg laying, incubation and hatching. Unlike earlier ornithologists, who had dismissed the clay-colored sparrow's call as a repetitious, insect-like drone, *bizz-bizz-bizz*, I identified varied sequences of one, two and three notes. I also heard a higher, more musical song, *bee-beez—beez-beez-beez*, and a low-pitched *zee-ze-zee*.

I had no difficulty getting close to the birds. I erected two small blinds made of saplings and sacking about two feet from the nests. The birds showed little nervousness and quickly accepted the blinds as part of their environment, frequently using them as a perch. The male was more nervous than the female, but soon ceased uttering his *tchip* alarm note after I had entered the blind. Twelve minutes after I entered, the female came to the nest with food.

I met Betsy Hauk in 1937, and we were married five years later.

I soon recognized the young birds' hungry *teep! teep!* calls for food, followed by a low, contented *tsee-tsee-tseet* when food arrived. I closely monitored the feeding and calculated that the four young consumed more than 1,300 insects in eight days, or 325 per bird. I was intrigued to discover that although grasshoppers were plentiful around the nest, the adult birds, apparently adhering to a feeding timetable, invariably flew off to fetch insects from a distance.

The Natural History Society of Manitoba, whose members included professors at the University of Manitoba, was impressed by my study of the clay-colored sparrow, and I was invited to present it at one of the society's weekly Monday-evening meetings. Giving a lecture was a daunting prospect. I was only twenty-five years old, and most of the talks were given by the professors, who would be in the audience. I decided to illustrate my talk with slides I prepared myself, using my own photos, graphs and tables, projected on an epidiascope, a primitive precursor to the overhead projector.

My talk was a success, and the following year, 1934, I was invited to lecture on hawks in Manitoba. This talk I illustrated with hand-painted cardboard slides showing the different species in adult and immature plumage. Hawks, especially the red-tailed hawk, were among my favorite birds, but predatory birds were so unpopular with the public that there was no market for hawk paintings.

For me, however, the hawk was a bird of good omen: it was at this lecture that I met seventeen-year-old Betsy Haak, who, five years later, would become my wife.

Ruffed Grouse in Poplar Woods
1956
oil on canvas board
18″ x 24″
Private collection

Poplar woods were a most suitable background for ruffed grouse. This painting gave me an opportunity to show both the male and female plumage of the species.

CHAPTER FIVE

Museum Work

In June 1934, my brother, Terry, invited me to accompany him on a two-week bird survey, funded by the Royal Ontario Museum, of the Lake St. Martin area, which lay between Lake Winnipeg and Lake Manitoba. The trip there took two days, and for the last stretch we rode in a two-horse wagon which, of course, had no springs.

We were met by Sam Waller, a missionary and schoolteacher on the Lake St. Martin Reserve. A bachelor in his thirties, Waller was much interested in natural history. Birds were his main study, and for some years he had been sending migration records, nesting data and specimens, taken by the people on the reserve, to the Royal Ontario Museum. It was as a result of his reports that we were sent to gather additional material for a museum presentation. Our headquarters were in his cottage, overlooking Lake St. Martin.

We spent long days in the field, scouting the marsh and surrounding territory on the west side of the lake. We also made one-day trips with a guide to Pine and Sugar islands. The latter was named for the Manitoba maple trees growing on it from which the native people extracted sap and made sugar.

We recorded 141 species of birds and filled in some gaps in the breeding range of a number of Manitoba birds. Though I did no sketching beyond one or two pencil drawings of the islands, I did take photographs of the various types of habitat, from marsh to forest. For me, the experience gained in the field and the opportunity

In 1934, I accompanied my brother, Terry, on a bird survey, funded by the Royal Ontario Museum, of the Lake St. Martin area, between Lake Winnipeg and Lake Manitoba. Our headquarters were the cottage of Sam Waller, shown here.

Terry and I spent many days scouting the marshes on the west side of the Lake St. Martin.

of seeing many birds first-hand in their natural surroundings, plus improving my skill at preparing skins, proved valuable in the next few years.

Coincidentally, after many years of disappointment, the Natural History Society of Manitoba's efforts to open a museum in Winnipeg were coming to fruition. In 1932, the imposing new Civic Auditorium had been built to house the museum, an art galley and two theaters. By late 1934 the museum was anxious to add bird and mammal exhibits. An expert technician was required if specimens were to be preserved and mounted in ways that looked reasonably lifelike.

I applied for the job and was hired immediately as artist technician. I started work on January 1, 1935, at a salary of seventy-five dollars a month. I was elated. My long wait had ended at last. Now I would be able to put to good use all that I had learned in those "lost years." Assisted by Bert Cartwright and Alex Lawrence, another Winnipeg birder friend, I set to work preparing a representative display of Manitoba birds.

In 1935, I carried out our plan of exhibiting as many Manitoba birds as we had available. These were, for the most part, a collection put together by George Atkinson, a taxidermist from Portage la Prairie. There were, though, many gaps in his collection, which I proceeded to fill as time permitted.

One attractive exhibit was a ruby-throated hummingbird's nest and a pair of adults. The nest had been donated, but we had no birds to go with it. I drew the line at shooting any of these little birds. Instead, I carved a pair out of balsa wood and used curved slivers of hardwood for the beaks. I painted them very carefully with oils, and before the paint was dry I dusted on metallic powder, which accented the glowing red throat and glossy green back of the male. For eyes, we used small black-headed pins. No one ever seemed to

The Eagle Through the Ages
1935
ink on paper board
12 ½" x 16 ⅛"
Collection of the artist

Bert Cartwright wrote the column "Wild Wings" for the Winnipeg Tribune*. I was interested in eagles and did this drawing to illustrate the history of the eagle in different cultures through the ages. I did it on spec at Bert's urging, with the idea that the Tribune might be interested in printing it. It was not used, however, because of cutbacks brought about by the Depression.*

doubt that they were real birds, and we had no trouble from moths or dermetid beetles, a terror on mounted birds.

The study and conservation of western Canadian birds was encouraged by the passage of the Migratory Bird Act. The Canadian government had belatedly realized that at least some species had to be protected from reckless, indiscriminate slaughter. J. Dewey Soper, the newly appointed chief migratory bird officer for the Prairie provinces, was renowned in naturalist circles for having discovered the nesting grounds of the blue and snow goose on Baffin Island in 1929. I, however, turned out to be the authority on Grant's Lake, a broad, deep marsh west of Winnipeg where every spring flocks of blue and snow geese landed to rest and feed on their long flight to the Arctic. I had visited Grant's Lake many times during these spring migrations, and I had given Dewey Soper copies of my field notes. On April 18, 1930, for instance, I had noted:

"As we neared the grounds, great flocks of geese covered the southern sky in formations of Vs, crescents and long, straggling lines, while thousands were circling over the prairie to the north, their calls echoing from all sides. An immense local flock, observed on a stubble field several hundred yards from our position, contained three or four thousand birds. As we were watching, they suddenly rose in a body and the noise of their wings beating rapidly in such numbers was astonishing in both tone and volume; to this was added the clamour of their calls and those of incoming flocks answering from all points of the sky as they circled and drifted down to join the legions already dotting the fields. The large flock, after rising about two hundred feet, circled the field in the bright sunlight, flashing black and white in a kaleidoscope pattern as they alighted again some distance away.

"Four other great flocks, noted farther off, surpassed in size the one described. One especially large company rose like a dark thundercloud in the distance, the main body of the birds constantly increasing in size as an endless stream of arrivals poured in. The blue and lesser snow geese congregate here for food and to recuperate after their long flight from the Gulf of Mexico. Arriving here about April 1, or a little later, the great flight of incoming birds lasts several days until it seems that practically all the blue and lesser snow geese on the North American continent had arrived. They remain for several weeks and suddenly, as if by some prearranged signal, they renew their flight to the northern breeding grounds. The blue geese are more numerous, outnumbering the lesser snow geese by about five to one."

To help prepare my 1935 exhibit of snow geese, I hired Bill Watkins, a former forester and a good shot. I required seven geese to create a diorama. Watkins and I were driven out to Grant's Lake by Betsy's brother, Adrian Haak. We stayed overnight in a hayloft, but slept little since the murmur of the geese continued throughout the night without pause. It was not the clamor of daytime, but rather a contented, reassuring sound.

At dawn, we were up and headed for the edge of the lake. It was foggy, and in the half-light the mist seemed to hang in the air above us. We could hear the calls of flocks in flight, and several passed overhead, in and out of the fog. As the sun rose, the fog dissipated and we could see geese in flight in all directions, their calls rising in volume. We had our seven geese in less than half an hour. We could not have done better had we had the opportunity to handpick the birds ourselves. The range in plumage in the three blue geese was exactly what we wanted. After eating our sandwiches, we walked to a ridge and sat down, content to watch the panorama of geese over and beyond the lake.

After mounting the geese in my workroom at the museum, I set to work painting a backdrop on sign painter's cloth stretched on a wood frame (canvas was beyond the museum's tiny budget). Using powdered colors and water, I painted an evening sky over Grant's Lake with a big cloud of geese rising over the water. I must have painted a thousand geese — small, mind you, with a two- or three-inch wingspan. In the foreground, I painted several geese on the ground with their heads raised, calling to others in flight.

For the floor of the case, I tacked a loose screen over a wooden frame and covered it with papier-mâché and plaster of Paris, which I colored to resemble earth. On top I placed clumps of prairie grass and clusters of prairie crocus made from crepe paper. When all the details were taken care of, the geese were added.

The workroom itself was a fascinating display of constantly changing works-in-progress. For a 1936 spring exhibit of Franklin's gulls at Grant's Lake, Bill Watkins volunteered to bag seven birds near the St. Boniface garbage dump, where he had seen them in flocks. I lent Watkins my shotgun, and he went to visit the dump.

The following morning I was busy in the preparation room when Bill walked in. It was typical Watkins — an old suit, a fedora with the brim turned down all around, Charlie Chaplin mustache, frowning black eyebrows and a look of concern on his face. He

In 1939, I found work as a technician in the Manitoba Museum. I set up many of the museum's displays, in addition to doing some taxidermy work. Here, I am in my work area surrounded by some of the birds I mounted.

was carrying a big canvas bag like the ones newsboys carried their daily papers in. I wondered what he had been up to.

"Lord God, Angus. Honest, I didn't mean to shoot so many," he said, unloading the bag on the floor. "I got ten!"

"That's all right, Bill. We can use them all," I replied. Then he told me how it had happened. He had collected five birds and was aiming at another taking off right in front of him. At the instant of firing, a whole flock rose into the air. Not only did he bag the bird he wanted, four more fell dead out of the flock. To

Pintails
1968
watercolor on board
9 $^{15}/_{16}$" x 12"
Collection of Jim Richardson, Winnipeg

My paintings of pairs of birds coming off the water were very popular with collectors. I varied the habitat and sometimes showed the birds lifting off and sometimes landing, often from different directions.

his credit, he retrieved them all and, wrapping them in newspaper, delivered them in excellent shape.

Mounting ten gulls was simple compared to the challenges presented by a golden eagle and a pinnated grouse, commonly known as a prairie chicken. The eagle, with a wingspan of 76 inches, was the largest bird I had ever mounted. I posed it at the moment of take-off, legs and feet down, wings full spread in the initial downward stroke as the bird lifts off. Heavy-gauge wire was necessary to give strength and rigidity. I paid particular attention to the widely spreading primary feathers of the wings; these curve upwards under the air pressure from the powerful downstroke. To achieve this curved position in the first five primaries of each wing, I inserted a wire into the base of each quill, securing the wire along the length of the tapering quill tip with duck cement. When dry and set, the wired feathers were bent to the desired curves. This great bird, gripping a 2" x 4" board in its spread claws, made quite a spectacle on the top of my workbench. When it was ready, we suspended it from the ceiling of one of the display cases by four thin wires.

With the pinnated grouse, I was concerned about the large inflatable sacs of skin located on each side of the neck of the male. These sacs are inflated during mating display until they resemble a couple of oranges. Their size, combined with the bright orange color, gives the bird a striking appearance as he struts about. Our bird had been found dead with the sacs fully inflated and sent to the museum. In the process of skinning, the sacs deflated and all efforts to reinflate them failed. Reluctant to stuff them with tow or cotton batten, as was generally done, I decided to use toy balloons. So on my lunch hour I stopped at Woolworth's and picked up a couple of five-cent balloons.

First, I cut out the sac. Then I inflated a balloon and inserted it, fitting it snugly and securing it in place. The fit was good and the effect realistic. For the coloring, I prepared a mixture of orange oil color and beeswax, thinned to be sprayed on the balloon with a fixative. Successive layers were built up until we had achieved the desired effect. It looked good. The dry wax shell had all the bright color and form of the inflated sacs with no wrinkling evident.

I visited the museum six years later and the beeswax was still holding up, colorful and smooth. Whether the balloon had any air in it remains a mystery.

Juvenile Black-capped Chickadee.
The Pas. Manitoba. June. 12. 1937.
Reader Lake.

A. H. Short
1937.

Juvenile Black-capped Chickadee
1937
watercolor on paper
5 $\frac{5}{16}$" x 5 $\frac{3}{8}$"
Collection of the artist

*This study was done at Reader Lake,
north of The Pas.*

CHAPTER SIX

The Study of Birds

?n the summer of 1937, Percy Taverner invited me to join him on a three-month-long survey of birds in The Pas and Swan River areas of north-western Manitoba. I was delighted by the opportunity to study birds in the field, and by Taverner's generous offer of $125 a month.

When we met for the first time, in Winnipeg on May 30, 1937, I found Taverner to be an engaging personality, tall and slim with white hair, a mustache and goatee. I had hired Bill Watkins as the expedition's cook, handyman and field assistant. Watkins knew little about birds, but his knowledge of forestry would be an asset in wooded areas, and I found him a congenial companion.

We set up our camp at Reader Lake, a fair-sized lake about sixteen miles north of The Pas. The shoreline varied from gently sloping mudflats to spruce and poplar forest. At the south end was an island and, farther south, a small river bordered by low, wet areas.

The island rose to a height of about fifty feet, and it was heavily overgrown with willow and poplar intermixed with spruce. The underbrush was thick and littered with fallen trees.

Our first morning we were up at six. It was cold! We were grateful for the warmth of the cookstove, which Taverner had going full blast. As he started to prepare bacon and eggs, I helped Watkins get the dishes and lay the table. In no time, the tempting aroma of coffee and frying bacon had us eager for breakfast. Then we had uninvited company — tent caterpillars! These creatures

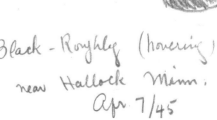

Pure white

Black - Roughleg (hovering)
near Hallock Minn.
Apr 7/45

descended on the area every ten or so years and completely defoliated the trees. Attracted to the heat of the chimney pipe, they were crawling down it in scores. Of course, when they reached a hot spot, they let go and came dropping down onto the stove, sizzling and popping like popcorn. Taverner, unperturbed, flipped them out of the pan and went on cooking.

At seven o'clock. Watkins and I set out with our guns, binoculars, cameras and a liberal supply of anti-mosquito dope, which we sorely needed. The first part of our tramp was pleasant, for we were in the open, along the shallow sedge-meadow border, where the wind kept the mosquitoes at bay. Then we came to a rough gravel and rock stretch of shoreline and had to go around it by entering the woods along the ridge. Here the mosquitoes were in clouds. We applied the dope liberally, a concoction recommended by Dewey Soper. He gave me the formula and I had it made up by our druggist: one ounce oil of citronella, one ounce spirits of camphor, one-half ounce oil of cedar and one ounce of sweet oil. It did contribute to a glorious tan. What it did to our shirt sleeves and collars can be imagined.

We made our way through the woods as quickly as we could. Tent caterpillars were especially bad in the poplar woods, where they were in such numbers they were rapidly defoliating the trees. Their webs were on everything and they made our progress difficult and slow. Then, to top it off, it started to rain. In a few minutes we were soaking wet. We continued on for about an hour until we reached a hill at the northeast corner of the lake. We had to climb over tumbled rocks to reach the top, thickly wooded with tall spruce, some birch and poplar. Here too the caterpillars were numerous, their webs, literally like curtains, spread everywhere on the underbrush. We made a circuit of the hill as best we could, but as it was now raining steadily we headed back to camp, dry clothes and a good lunch with canned sausages as the main course.

After lunch we covered the tabletop with newspapers and got to work preparing the bird specimens taken on our morning round. This occupied us until four o'clock, when, the rain having ceased and the sun shining, Watkins and I ventured out again. We kept to the edge of the spruce-poplar woods along the southeastern border of the lake, but the mosquitoes were thick. We really plastered on the dope, but it was most uncomfortable trying to use binoculars or cameras when the insects were in such numbers around our faces and hands.

Towards dusk, three yellow rails, small marsh birds, were heard calling at intervals. Their notes were given in a series of five, with a slight pause following the opening two: *tick-tick — tick-tick-tick*. I realized that a specimen would be a valuable addition to our collection, so, accompanied by Watkins, I headed for the location, sedge bordering the lake in shallow water. We tramped back and forth across the area, flushing single birds into flight. Their brief appearance as they fluttered zigzag fashion just above the sedge gave us the nearest glimpse we had of them, and although we got in a couple of shots, they eluded us. On the third attempt, I bagged one with my twelve-gauge shotgun just as the light was fading. It proved to be a northern record for the species.

Although I had never camped out in the bush before, I was optimistic about the work and stoic about the hardships of field research. But Percy Taverner, a veteran of numerous collecting expeditions, was more irritated than he let on. In his own field notes, he complained that the deep, sticky mud of the lake bed made it impossible for "the boys," as he called Watkins and me, to approach the flocks of waders and waterbirds far out on the flats, and he secretly found "disgusting" the plague of tent caterpillars.

As for my prize yellow rail, Taverner noted on June 4: "Last night the boys went after the yellow rails. I heard a great fusillade and presently they came in with one yellow rail and a nighthawk, both shot after dusk. The rails flushed for them quite readily and several times, but always very close and down again almost immediately. When they did get it, they blew it pretty well to pieces — one side and wing completely off. I did the best I could with the fragments."

The following days continued to be plagued by mosquitoes, but we were successful in recording many species, including olive-sided and least flycatchers; magnolia, Tennessee, chestnut-sided and Canada warblers; a sharp-shinned hawk, purple finch and house wren; a greater yellowlegs; a sharp-tailed sparrow; and a Nelson's sparrow, a northern record for the species.

After a few days, we moved our camp to Halcrow Lake, three miles south of The Pas. The lake was surrounded by marsh and appeared more suited to waterbirds. Three new species were recorded while we worked setting up tents and unpacking. A Wilson's snipe gave a wonderful performance of its "winnowing" flight overhead, alternately flying upwards then diving at a steep angle, the winnowing sound evidently produced by the fanning of tail feathers and the rush of air through them.

Our first exploration was the woods behind our camp, largely black poplar with some fine old trees fifty to sixty feet high. In the poplars we sighted mourning warblers and cedar waxwings, the latter a new addition to our list. As we worked our way to the north end of the marsh we came into more open country, marshy with dry ridges of grass and willow thickets.

As part of our bird survey in northwestern Manitoba in the summer of 1937, we spent a few days at Halcrow Lake. For the early part of the survey, Percy Taverner, our leader, did much of the cooking in camp kitchens like this one. Bill Watkins is on the left and I am on the right.
June 16, 1937.

Sprague's Pipit. Imm.
Garland, Manitoba.
July. 29. 1937.

a. H. Shortt
1 9 3 7.

Sprague's Pipit (Immature)
1937
watercolor on paper
5 ½" x 7"
Collection of the artist

This field study was done when we were at Garland, Manitoba. This species is rare and has been compared to an old country skylark.

Here were clay-colored sparrows, alder flycatchers and northern yellowthroats. The sun was very warm and the sky cloudless, a perfect day for wading about in the marsh. Marsh birds were plentiful, including dowitchers, eared grebes, black terns and many ducks, canvasbacks and lesser scaups.

Six days later we headed for the Pasquia River and worked south along the east side to where we had seen the terns. On a small pond beside the river there was a flock of mallards, nearly all male, that I estimated at two hundred birds. A few American wigeon and northern shoveler drakes were among them. While exploring a patch of mud and bulrush for snipe, a tern flew over me and was shot. It proved to be a Forster's tern.

Heading back, we were crossing a small grassy stretch when I was astonished to hear the flight song of a Sprague's pipit, the North American counterpart of the old country skylark. A careful search of the sky overhead revealed two singing males, up almost beyond binocular range. I watched one for twenty-two minutes. It was still in the air singing when I spotted another diving to earth. We secured a specimen a few minutes later, our first record and only northern record for the species.

On June 20, we woke to a cool morning with a heavy dew and mist rising over the lake. Taverner advised us that he planned to move camp the next day and head for Swan River, about 180 miles to the south. He felt that we had done a thorough job of The Pas area. I said I would like to try one more time to collect a specimen of the Connecticut warbler. He was quite in agreement.

Watkins and I left camp about eight in the morning and headed for the black spruce bog. We had no luck in the area where we had encountered them on our previous two visits. We heard no singing males. Disappointed, we were on our way back, trudging through wet sphagnum in the warm sun, when I located a singing male in a new area on our right. The song was given off at regular intervals, and although it was loud and clear, I knew it was some distance off.

Deciding on a final effort, we headed in the direction of the song. It was hard going, but suddenly the song was given from the dense undergrowth at no great distance from us. I motioned to Watkins, and we both crouched down among the moss, quietly waiting. When we next heard his song, he was in one of three tall spruces not twenty feet above our heads. After a tense few minutes, there was a slight movement at the top of the tallest tree. I then had a glimpse of the bird moving among a small cluster of cones. A quick shot and our quest was ended.

It was a splendid specimen, and I made a pencil sketch in spite of the flies, mosquitoes and heat. For Taverner, this bird, the yellow rail and the Sprague's pipit were the highlights of the trip.

A few days later Taverner told me he planned to leave for Ottawa on the evening of June 25. He sat for some time outlining the additional camps and areas Watkins and I were to explore as we moved south. I was to correspond with him in Ottawa, and he would advise on dates for moving camps.

Taverner's own field notes offer no explanation for his abrupt, unexpected departure after less than four weeks into a twelve-week survey. Perhaps, at age sixty-two, he was feeling too old for the rigors of a summer in the bush. It was supposed to be Watkins's job to cook, not Taverner's, but while Watkins and I were slogging for miles through bogs and deadfall, Taverner seems to have rarely, if ever, left the immediate vicinity of the campsite. His eyesight was failing — he identified birds first by their songs — and his notes make clear that after two

Here, I am crouching on top of one of the trees blown down during the terrible storm at Swan River on July 10, 1937. I'm carrying my 410, the gun I used to obtain my museum specimens.

weeks in the field, he had learned to respect the abilities of his young assistant. On June 14, Taverner wrote:

"A day or so ago, Shortt declared he had seen a Virginia rail, but it seemed so improbable that I did not take it very seriously. This afternoon, just before supper, I saw a swamp sparrow in the reeds in front of camp. However, it evidently disappeared in the dead reeds. I stood watching for it and began to squawk to draw it into the open. At almost the first squawk, I saw a rail in the distance rise from the marsh and fly a short distance towards me. A moment later it rose again, nearer still, and approached another step. Then all at once I saw it in the grass at the edge of the marsh, almost at my feet. It was a Virginia rail. Rapidly backing off, I shot it. Certainly a northern record for this species. Shortt made a drawing of the head and bill."

Watkins and I continued on without Taverner for the rest of the summer. We faced many long, hot days and one terrific storm, but the weeks were full of wonderful moments and splendid sights. By the end of August, the leaves were beginning to turn color and the birds, already beginning their southern migration, were becoming scarcer. Our final days we spent checking over and packing our specimens, writing up reports and preparing our equipment for shipment on the train to Winnipeg.

It had been a hard summer, but a successful one. During our eighty-three days in the field, Watkins and I recorded a total of 161 species. It was a high point in my study of birds. I not only became acquainted with them on their nesting grounds but had the opportunity to study avian anatomy first hand by preparing scientific specimens. It was a valuable training obtainable nowhere else.

Despite the summer's successes, I returned to bad news. The Manitoba Museum was facing bankruptcy. On February 7, 1938, I wrote a bleak letter to Taverner: "I am much disappointed with the prospects here. Since the Carnegie Foundation withdrew their financial assistance, there seems no hope of steady employment. I wonder if you could advise me as to possible contacts to the south in respect to preparatory work. I have prepared a folder with photographs of my work and original samples of drawings and watercolors of mammals, birds, flowers, frogs and insects with the idea of submitting it to various museums in hope of obtaining a position as assistant."

My hopes were dashed by Taverner's reply: "Too bad that you have not been able to build up enough interest to keep up the museum on the lapse of the Carnegie fund. . . . I can well understand your looking to the States for a possible museum position. But the

Belted Kingfisher ♀
Swan River, Manitoba.
July 14. 1937.

a. H. Shortt.
1 9 3 7.

Belted Kingfisher (Female)
1937
watercolor on paper
8 ³/₁₆″ x 5 ³/₄″
Collection of the artist

*I completed this field study at Swan River.
It was unusual to find this bird there
because they often stay in treed areas.
I was interested in the pattern in its
feathers, the shape of its head and
its coloring.*

American museums are mostly all fully staffed and are too pinched by the depressive conditions to expand. . . . I fear that your artistic ability, while a decided asset, is not a determinative one as there are more good bird artists appearing than there is call for them. . . . However, there is no chance of such connection unless you make application. Go to it. But I advise you to get a good steady job at anything that promises in the meantime."

Taverner did ask me if I might be available for another field survey the next summer. I replied: "Would be glad to go if chosen. I hardly expect employment here after May, unless something unusual happens with our grants." To my relief, Taverner hired me, with a new young assistant, Richard Sutton, to conduct a bird survey of the Dauphin area, including Riding Mountain National Park, from May 15 to September 15, 1938.

Then, only days before I was to leave for Dauphin, the American Museum of Natural History offered me a four-month contract, with possible extensions, at a salary of $125 a month. I would start work September 1. I leapt at this opportunity to work at a national museum with ambitious projects, a big budget and a large, skilled staff, and Taverner generously allowed me to wrap up his field trip a month early. The bird survey was a success — 83 species recorded at Dauphin, 115 at Clear Lake in Riding Mountain National Park.

When I returned to Winnipeg in mid-August, I felt so elated that I asked Betsy to marry me. A week later, I left for New York. It was going to be hard to leave Betsy, Winnipeg and the west, but I had high hopes of getting into painting in New York, perhaps assisting with background work on some large dioramas, which were then in vogue.

After the summer survey, I was offered a job at the Museum of Natural History in New York City. The work wasn't as exciting as I had hoped, but I enjoyed seeing the sights of the city, such as Central Park, seen here. October 16, 1938.

On arriving at the museum, however, I was disappointed to find myself assigned to the taxidermy department, with no immediate prospect of painting, and even more dismayed when I was put to work softening old vulture skins for a new diorama in the African exhibit. The vultures had been skinned in the field and preserved with arsenic and a salt mixture. We placed them in a bin of moist sawdust to loosen the skin. Then we worked on the inside of the skin with scalpel and tweezers, freeing the base of each feather and cleaning away all cartilage and sinew until the feathers were loose and pliable. This was a slow, painstaking job as some of the skins were more than ten years old.

After preparing the smelly vultures for mounting, I was assigned to prepare and mount an exhibit of South Pacific petrels in flight. I hadn't finished the petrels when I was handed a wandering albatross to "loosen up." It was a twenty-year-old skin. The bird was as big as a pelican with a wingspan of eleven feet! It was to be mounted in full flight, so all the wing feathers had to be limbered up. I wrestled with this big flying machine for two weeks, slowly separating upwards of one hundred flight feathers, as well as other feathers. Finally I got it done. Thankfully, it was near Christmas and I was going home for the holidays.

Difficult and unpleasant as I often found the work, I was pleased when the museum extended my contract for another three months. During that time I managed to meet with the museum's famous diorama painter, Francis Lee Jaques, and I was introduced to Charles R. Knight, a museum artist renowned for his paintings of dinosaurs.

Knight was a friendly, white-haired man in his sixties. One day he came into the preparation room and stopped to chat with me for a few minutes. My superior, John Potter, showed him some of my work. He was more interested than I expected, and he ended by giving me some sage advice. Reaching into one of his waistcoat pockets, he brought out the stub of a pencil not more than two inches long. "This," he said, "is what I do my sketching with. It's a soft pencil; it gives you a strong outline to start with." It was sound advice, and I have since found that I can sketch more accurately with a soft, short pencil, although mine are not less than four inches long.

It was, however, a precarious livelihood. I had taken with me a portfolio of my sketches and paintings of birds, but although the museum staff had admired my work — Potter bought two, a ruffed grouse and a purple finch — no offer of work as an artist was forthcoming. Instead, it was my mentor, Bert Cartwright, recently hired as chief field naturalist for Ducks Unlimited Canada, a new organization starting up in Winnipeg, who, at Christmas, gave me my longed-for opportunity to become a professional artist.

Pintails
1949
oil on canvas
20 ³/₁₆" x 24 ⅛"
Collection of Mr. and Mrs. Bill Leitch, Winnipeg

Bill Leitch, who was head biologist for Ducks Unlimited Canada for thirty-eight years, commissioned this painting. It's one of my early oils and shows how my style changed later.

CHAPTER SEVEN

Ducks Unlimited

I was familiar with Ducks Unlimited. I had already designed the letterhead for their Winnipeg office, and the past spring, I had accompanied engineer D. M. Stevens, on loan from Manitoba Hydro, on a two-day survey of what remained of Big Grass Marsh, eighty miles northwest of Winnipeg on the western shore of Lake Manitoba, a location that Ducks Unlimited had chosen as its first restoration project in Manitoba.

The whole area had once been a marsh and had supported vast wildlife. The first European settlers found a shallow 100,000-acre lake fringed by rushes that grew more than ten feet tall. Photographs show settlers paddling and sailing on Big Lake, as they called it. But in 1885 the Manitoba government undertook to drain marshlands so these low-lying areas could be sold to homesteaders. Ditches were dug throughout the Red River Valley. In spite of disturbing signals — farms that, by midsummer, were bone dry — drainage, like clearing and cultivating woodlots, became an article of unquestioned faith. *The Gladstone Age Press* of Gladstone, Manitoba, exulted: "It has long been recognized that this drained land is among the most valuable in the province, for it possesses a store of crop-producing elements which appear inexhaustible. While the sportsmen of the province have lost a grand duck shooting ground, the province has gained thousands of acres of land which will produce returns on a valuation of millions of dollars."

But soon the wells began to run dry. The Big Grass farmers dug deeper wells. They too went dry. Big Grass Marsh had become a desert on which no crops would grow.

Then came the drought of the 1930s, which not only further dried up the already parched land but caused wildlife populations to plummet. These events awoke Canadian and American sportsmen to the fact that without quality habitat there would be no abundance of waterfowl. In 1937, a group of them formed Ducks Unlimited to restore and preserve the wetlands and protect the ducks' habitat.

When Stevens and I arrived at Big Grass in 1938, we met one farmer who had already built a crude, homemade dam across the marsh's main drainage ditch, and to our surprise, the center of the marsh held water. We drove to several points around the marsh's perimeter, then donned our hip waders and investigated the aquatic food and cover growth for its value to waterfowl. It had great potential as a nesting area. We recorded flocks of blue and snow geese and five small flocks of Canada geese. Ducks were plentiful, but widely dispersed. The principal species were pintail, mallard, shoveler, blue-winged teal and wigeon. We observed eight sandhill cranes in flight towards the north end of the marsh. Local residents told us the cranes sometimes nested in the area.

We saw nine pairs of marsh hawks. One male was sitting on a road, tearing a garter snake to pieces. When we approached, the hawk took wing with the remains of the snake dangling from his talons. Two males, at separate locations, were performing their aerial courtship flights, carrying out the stoops and zooms at low altitude. One bird at the top of a zoom, perhaps fifty feet up, plummeted earthward and came up with a meadow vole in his claws.

When Bert Cartwright offered me a job as a field naturalist with Ducks Unlimited, I hesitated. I enjoyed field work, but would I have any opportunities to paint? Well, yes, Ducks Unlimited was setting up a public relations department. The next day, after an interview with Ducks Unlimited manager Tom Main, I was hired at a salary of $135 a month. I started work on January 2, 1939. I was happy to be again in the west, close to the marshes and woods I loved so well and, above all, with Betsy.

Betsy and I set our wedding date for March 17. Our marriage, after five years of courtship, was a quiet family ceremony in the manse of Norwood United Church.

Ducks Unlimited in Winnipeg was such a small organization that I found myself working closely not only with Cartwright but with the director of public relations, irrepressible Ed Russenholt, and the engineer, George Fanset. Our first daunting task was to arrive at an accurate estimate of the numbers and locations of the summer waterfowl population in all three prairie provinces. Questionnaires were mailed to about two thousand "keemen," farmers and ranchers primarily, who reported on duck populations and water conditions in their areas in spring, summer and fall. It fell to me to draw maps and charts illustrating the information gleaned from these reports.

I also took part in surveys to examine existing marsh areas. Early in the summer of 1939, George Fanset and I made a preliminary survey of the great Saskeram marshes west of The Pas along the Saskatchewan River. Later, I returned for a more extensive examination of marsh conditions and duck populations, accompanied by a Russian biologist, Dr. Alexander Bajkov. An expert on freshwater fish, Bajkov was to evaluate the predation of northern pike on duck populations.

The Russian biologist Dr. Alexander Bajkov accompanied us on the Ducks Unlimited survey to The Pas in 1939 to assess the predation of northern pike on duck populations.

We focused our attention on the Summerberry and Cumberland marshes. The Summerberry was our first objective. This complex of small, marshy lakes and creeks lies east of The Pas and north of the Saskatchewan River. A Manitoba government boat let us off at Little Fish Lake. Here we made our headquarters in game warden Jack Heard's log cabin, and Jack took us to several other marshy lakes during our stay.

While I concentrated on waterfowl counts, Bajkov fished at every opportunity. He caught a fair number of pike, and a number of these contained duckling remains. One had eaten a young muskrat.

Later, we traveled up the Saskatchewan River to the Cumberland Marsh by canoe with two Indian guides. For many years, the Hudson's Bay Company post at Cumberland House had operated a lucrative muskrat-trapping project in the area. The company had built a large rock-and-timber dam to regulate water levels throughout the area. However, the dam had deteriorated over the years and no longer served its purpose. Rather than rebuild it, the company let it collapse. Ducks Unlimited was interested in controlling the water level in the area for waterfowl. Within the area, a number of small lakes, Swan, Cut Beaver, Bloodsucker, Egg and Red Earth, were connected by a maze of creeks and channels with abundant aquatic duck food plants and excellent nesting cover for a variety of ducks.

The marshes were superior to any I had ever seen. The surfaces of many creeks were covered with lily pads, and we would frequently see a red-winged blackbird or rail go scampering across them from one side to the other. The duck population was good, although I had expected to see more species.

My delight in the Cumberland marshes, however, was marred by frequent headaches, blurred vision and painful flashes of light in my right eye. On my return, an ophthalmologist diagnosed a progressive traumatic cataract, likely the consequence of a blow to the eye. I recalled being hit across the eye by a branch on one of my earlier field trips, but after a day or two the eye had seemed fine.

White-winged and Surf Scoters
1982
graphite on paper
16" x 21"
Collection of Mrs. Jean Moermond, Midland, Minnesota

Before I begin a painting, I draw the outlines of the shapes and make color notes on the drawing for future reference. I changed the final oil a little by repositioning a couple of the birds and adding two more.

White-winged, Surf and Common Scoters
April 1983
oil on canvas board
18" x 24"
Collection of Mrs. Jean Moermond, Midland, Minnesota

I have sometimes done paintings of species I've seen in only photographs in locations I haven't visited. For this painting, I placed these west coast birds in China Poot Bay, Alaska.

No operation was advised, as the vision in my left eye was 100 per cent, and no glasses could synchronize my sight. It was recommended that I wear glasses with a dark lens over the injured eye to alleviate the bright flashes of light I was experiencing when in sunlight. In due course the eye became totally blind, but all pain disappeared and I could wear my normal glasses.

I didn't allow my partial blindness to interfere with my determination to make my way as an artist. Beginning in June 1939, one of my tasks at Ducks Unlimited was to cut the stencil for a one-page report on waterfowl conditions distributed during the summer months to about fifteen hundred DU supporters and media outlets in Canada and the United States. In July 1940, this report was named the *Duckological*. In *Ducks and Men*, his history of Ducks Unlimited Canada, W. G. (Bill) Leitch, DU's retired chief biologist, writes: "While no one is entirely sure where the name came from, the general consensus is that it was from Ed Russenholt, after a brainstorming session in which many suggestions were bounced around. The *Duckological* combined and digested information on waterfowl and habitat from every available source: reports from keemen and fieldmen, weather reports, data from aerial surveys and sporadic reports from interested individuals. In its early years, the *Duckological* sparkled with Russenholt's clever caricatures. The *Ducko*, as it became known, was signed by whoever happened to be in the office to compile it. The day the *Duckological* went out — "Ducko Day" — was always exciting."

The *Ducko* was printed in the office on a hand-cranked Gestetner. I recall one Saturday when we were well into a run, Tom Main arrived back from an inspection trip out west. Ed Russenholt showed him a copy.

My wife, Betsy, took this photograph of me sitting on the riverbank near Rainbow Falls in the Whiteshell in 1946. I was sketching a great blue heron that was stalking a fish on the opposite rocky shore.

Sandhill Cranes

1944
watercolor on paper
15 ⁹/₁₆" x 22 ³/₈"
Collection of Drs. Ronald and Mithra Davey, Winnipeg

*This painting was done for Winnipeg collector
Jim Morton, who had a large collection of my early
works. Since these birds nest in many parts of
Manitoba, I made the background very general.*

Ruddy Turnstone
1944
watercolor on paper
10 $^7/_{16}$" x 15 $^3/_{16}$" (sight)
Private collection

When I began to take commissions, my clients often wanted to see the birds in their natural habitat. These shore birds have an upturned bill used to turn over stones and seaweed when feeding.

Because of the severe drought conditions in southern Alberta and southwestern Saskatchewan, it had simply the one word "Drought" printed across that area on the map.

"Rosie," Tom said, "it's more than drought; it's dry as hell!"

"Okay, Tom," Ed replied. "Let's put that on the map!"

So I went back to the drawing board and prepared a new map with the wording "Dry As Hell" printed in bold letters across the affected areas.

In 1940, Ed Russenholt put me to work on an imaginative fund-raising project. It was a prospectus titled "The Lake That Waits," which presented, in photographs and text, data on duck marshes available for restoration, with the provision that the sponsors could put their own chosen names to the areas when restoration was completed.

Our first presentation was a 14" x 12" ten-page folio. The covers were dark green cloth hardboard with "The Lake That Waits" printed in gold across the front. Inside, a selection of photos, a typed description of the area and a detailed map were mounted on ten sheets of art paper. There was also a breakdown of estimated costs to improve or restore the marsh. I added ornamentation to the pages with watercolor sketches of ducks and marsh plants.

The response was far beyond our expectations, and this donor program continued to be my primary work right up to my retirement in 1973. In its final form, the brochure was a hardcover, twelve-page, spiral-bound presentation. The color of the covers — green, blue, gray or burgundy — was chosen to match the lettering, which I did by hand in a variety of styles. As an added touch, I painted a pair of ducks, standing, sitting or, most often, in flight, on the covers. The species chosen was one that was popular in the flyway where the donor was located: mallard, for instance, for the Mississippi flyway; pintail or wigeon for the Pacific flyway. I would often have half a dozen of these colorful brochures in various stages of completion on my drawing table.

Learning to paint ducks was a challenge. Bird subjects most in demand with the public were small birds — blue jays, chickadees, grosbeaks — but by 1941, I was finding a growing market for my work among duck hunters. I embarked on a series of watercolor paintings of pairs of ducks, often in flight, on 12" x 14" sheets of rough-surfaced artist's paper. I did these at home, on my own time, and displayed them in the Ducks Unlimited office.

One day, a painting of a pair of canvasbacks caught Tom Main's eye, and he proposed that Ducks Unlimited buy the painting as a gift for the retiring president, W. C. Fisher of Calgary. Fisher's gift established a precedent: until my own retirement, every retiring DU president was presented with one of my duck paintings. Tom Main was so enthusiastic about my work that, in lieu of a salary increase, he gave me Fridays off so I would have more time to paint.

Magazines, too, were printing more color illustrations, and in 1945, I received one of my most important and popular commissions. *Sports Afield* magazine, published in Minneapolis, Minnesota, asked Bert Cartwright and me to produce illustrated profiles of thirty-six

Just before my retirement from Ducks Unlimited in 1973, I put the finishing touches on another twelve-page donor project brochure. The brochures were begun as a fund-raising idea. Each included photos and text about marshes that were available for restoration or development. Projects were often named after donors who sponsored them.

species of waterfowl to be published at the rate of one per month. I was to prepare a full-page color plate of birds in flight, plus a black-and-white wash drawing of the birds on the water to accompany Cartwright's text. A two-color map of North America that I drew would show nesting and wintering ranges.

The first painting, of mallards, appeared in *Sports Afield* in September 1945. More than three years later, the series was printed as a deluxe book, *Know Your Ducks and Geese*. In 1954, *Know Your Ducks and Geese*, which had gone through three printings, was republished in a $125 folio edition, each plate separate and suitable for framing, and as an inexpensive pocket-sized field guide.

Bluebills, Lake Francis Marsh, Manitoba
1963
oil on canvas board
17 $^7/_8$" x 23 $^{15}/_{16}$"
Collection of Richard Bonnycastle, Calgary

Migrating birds sometimes arrive even before the last snow has disappeared from the ground. Bluebills, also known as lesser scaup, migrate from as far away as northern South America.

Loons at Dawn
June 1985
oil on canvas board
18" x 24"
Collection of Rev. John Freeman, Winnipeg

I painted this as a gift for our minister and his late wife. Although I painted many pictures of loons with a similar background, this is the only pair I painted.

Gray Partridge in Snow
1970
oil on canvas board
17 $^7/_8$" x 23 $^7/_8$"
Collection of Mr. and Mrs. Duncan Jessiman, Winnipeg

Duncan Jessiman had a business and warehouse at the edge of the city near a prairie habitat and used to see these birds frequently. Gray partridge was an introduced species into selected areas of Canada and the United States.

CHAPTER EIGHT

An Artistic Career

My first artist's studio had been the spare bedroom in our St. Vital bungalow. I kept the door closed and splattered paint about as I pleased. Then, after our son, Terry, was born in 1947, I built a spacious studio on the back of the house. When, as Terry grew, the studio space was needed as a family room, I retreated upstairs to the attic, climbing up and down on a ladder that could be raised and lowered through the trapdoor. I was, literally, an artist in a garret — but not a starving one.

A breakthrough in my artistic career came in 1952, when several American directors of the parent corporation, Ducks Unlimited Inc., came to DU Canada's annual meeting in Winnipeg. Tom Main asked me to exhibit some of my paintings before the meeting. I chose five oils: three 16" x 20" canvases of pairs of ducks in flight — mallard, pintail and green-winged teal — and two 24" x 30" paintings, one show-

ing Canada geese coming in to a field of stooked grain, the other a flight of canvasbacks at Delta marsh, a popular hunting spot on Lake Manitoba. To my surprise, I sold four paintings. From this beginning, I built up a steady market among Ducks Unlimited members throughout the United States.

From my mother, I had learned to compose my pictures by first sketching the featured birds on tracing paper. After the backgrounds were dry, I positioned the tracings on the painting until I had arranged all the birds to my satisfaction. I then traced each outline and, working on one bird at a time, painted in the body. I started with the upper

King Eider
1950
watercolor on paper
14 $^3/_8$" x 10 $^5/_8$" (sight)
Private collection

This unusual-looking bird nests over much of the Arctic. It spends most of its time at sea and nests along the nearby shoreline.

Mallards over a Stooked Grain Field, Manitoba
1952
oil on canvas
24" x 30"
Collection of Mr. and Mrs. Donald S. Paterson, Winnipeg

This autumn scene shows a flock of startled mallards turning and flying away. The harvesting technique of stooking bundles of grain stalks to dry them hasn't been used for many decades in this area.

Canvasbacks, Netley Marshes, Lake Winnipeg
1951
oil on canvas
24" x 30 ¹/₄"
Collection of Mr. and Mrs. Hartley Richardson, Winnipeg

*This view was a favorite of collectors. In the various
paintings I did, I enjoyed changing the weather
conditions and the placement of the birds.*

wing, then did the head and neck and added the shadow on the body. Then I did the lower wing. The fine details, the eyes and feet were done last, after the rest was dry. I used opaque white to highlight the feathers. The foreground and any extra details were added at the very end.

Ironically, just as I was becoming adept at small watercolors, public taste was changing, and big pictures were coming into vogue. They were too big for watercolor, so I learned to paint in oils. You have to know which colors to mix, so I experimented. For my skies, I liked cobalt blue better than Prussian blue. It gives more of a bright sunlight effect. For clouds, I put the white in and tinted the shadows in the cloud. It's extremely difficult to get that correct. I finally found a color called Payne's gray. It looks black on its own, but mixed with white, it looks beautiful. I rarely used black.

Authenticity was important to me. I'd take a photograph of a marsh and make lots of notes about the colors. Then I'd go home and sketch it and experiment with washes for the colors of the different skies. I could also compose a picture from memory. I liked to go out evenings and mornings, twilight and dawn. I found the mixture of colors intriguing. I liked to photograph wheat fields with swaths of grain under evening skies —

Canvasbacks in Stormy Weather

1983
oil on canvas board
18 ¹/₁₆″ x 24″
Collection of George Cotter, Winnipeg

Here, I tried to capture the effect of high winds and rain on duck habitat. It's interesting to compare it with a similar scene on the facing page.

Orioles
1974
oil on canvas board
24″ x 11 ¹/₂″
Collection of Jim and Ann May

Neighbors across the street had a poplar tree in their back yard in which orioles had built a nest. It was such an interesting shape that they commissioned this painting.

Tundra Swans at Sunrise
1962
oil on canvas board
18″ x 24″
Collection of Alex and Jeanette Warga, Winnipeg

Over the years I painted many views of swans. At one time we called them whistling swans. I often painted different skies, like this one of a sunset.

Ross' Geese
1963
watercolor on paper board
10 $\frac{1}{16}$" x 12"
Collection of Mrs. Alice Patterson, London, Ontario

I painted this for a friend of Betsy's who liked Ross' geese. I put them in their nesting habitat on the tundra in the far north.

Bald Eagle and Osprey

1986
oil on canvas board
27 $^{15}/_{16}$" x 21 $^{15}/_{16}$"
Collection of Mr. and Mrs. Jim Bake,
Winnipeg

*I painted several versions of this scene,
all with slight variations. It shows a bald
eagle frightening an osprey. The eagle
forces the osprey to release the fish
and then catches it.*

15-cent Canada geese stamp

1963
corner block of four
envelope signed by the artist
Collection of Mr. Kasimir Bileski, Winnipeg

This Canadian postage stamp was designed after one of my paintings. My large oil painting was done for a special exhibit on nature art put on by the Natural History Society of Manitoba at the Hudson's Bay Company Store in 1949.

scenes in which the colors blended. I put reeds in the foreground and trees in the distance. Once I found that people liked the backgrounds, I made them more prominent.

David Hatch, an expert birder and my friend for fifty years, once said, "One thing that strikes me tremendously is that Angus will have a species in its proper habitat. Even if he has a very simple species with a little bit of water in the background, he'll still have the right kind of vegetation for the species, right down to the seeds. If it's a picture of evening grosbeaks, he knows what kind of food evening grosbeaks eat, so he puts them in an ash tree with the leaves all in fall colors and the seeds. If it's a fall scene of canvasbacks, the cattails are in their fall colors and they're all faded. The canvasbacks look like they do in the fall. Angus knows the bird, he knows the habitat and he'll harmonize the whole scene. Many, many people will paint the bird in a plumage different than the background indicates."

In 1949, I had painted a 32" x 40" work of four Canada geese in flight high over marshlands: the birds'-eye view creates the illusion that the viewer is flying with the geese. The painting was exhibited as part of a nature display in the Bay's Portage Avenue store.

When, more than ten years later, Betsy suggested to me that I submit a Canada goose design to the post office for a stamp, I chose the 1949 goose painting. I sent in a

CANADA GEESE in flight over Canadian Northlands . . . from a painting by the noted wildlife artist, Angus Shortt.

CANADIAN BANK NOTE CO., LIMITED.
OTTAWA Nº 2

K. BILESKI
Station B, Winnipeg

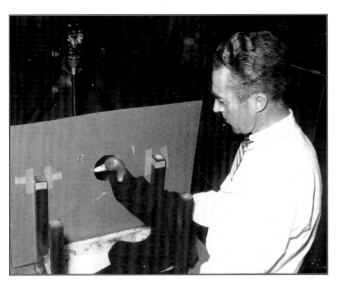

In 1950, I worked on the Ducks Unlimited movie "Meet the Ducks". For the animated sequences we took one frame at a time. Here, I am moving a carved wooden duck head for the titles at the beginning of the film.

For the film "Meet the Ducks," we photographed a map showing the flyways of ducks in North America.

detailed 9" x 12" pencil drawing with a letter pointing out some facts about Canada geese, stressing their wide appeal across Canada. I also offered to paint it in full color for color reproduction. To our surprise, the design was approved, and the pencil drawing was sufficiently detailed for the engraver. No color reproduction was contemplated.

In addition to my work at Ducks Unlimited, I helped George Cotter write and research his popular wildlife films. I assisted in preparing scripts, provided some hand-lettered titles and checked that the subject matter was correctly identified. Most outstanding was the 1944 movie "The Big Marsh Lives Again," the story of Ducks Unlimited's successful restoration of the Big Grass Marsh in western Manitoba.

In 1946, the Natural History Society of Manitoba awarded me its bronze medal for original research and artistic merit in ornithology, and in 1947, I was elected to the prestigious American Ornithologists' Union. I wrote "Wild Wings" column in the *Winnipeg Tribune* after Bert Cartwright retired, and I contributed illustrations to several Manitoba government publications, *Wildlife Crusader*, the *Wildlife Conservation Digest* and *Game Birds and Animals in Manitoba*, but my primary educational work was with Ducks Unlimited.

In 1970 a high priority was a Ducks Unlimited brochure that told the story of DU and set out the organization's plans and aims for the future. The text, with photographs, covered one half of one side of the sheet. On the other half, a map of North America showed waterfowl breeding grounds in Canada and the southward migration routes down the four major flyways into the United States. The reverse side of the sheet had illustrations of twenty-two species of ducks found across Canada.

The map and illustrations were my responsibility. The paintings, the ducks all in flight, I did on 8 1/2" x 11" watercolor board. For the map I used sheets of colored acetate overlays to denote the relative density of breeding pairs from the prairies northward. The brochure had an immediate, widespread appeal, especially in the schools. It went into three printings and the duck plates into five printings, lastly as an aid to field identification.

The success of the brochure and an increase in DU's budget presented me with a new challenge, "Marsh World," a series of black-and-white illustrations, with text, that Ducks Unlimited would distribute free to newspapers and periodicals. I was to produce one "Marsh World" a week, writing the text as well as drawing the birds in pen and ink. Contracted to continue the series after I retired, I produced 112 drawings over the next ten years. By the time "Marsh World" ended in 1981, my illustrations had appeared in more than eight hundred publications, many in French.

In September 1972, I received an unexpected assignment: Ducks Unlimited wanted me to devote my year before retirement entirely to painting. I could work at home, and a replacement artist would work on my other tasks. It was a dream come true. I quickly got down to the task, and in twelve months produced forty paintings ranging in size from 18" x 24" to 22" x 30". I did something for each flyway, flocks of canvasback, mallard, northern pintail, wigeon, blue-winged and green-winged teal, scaup, black duck, Canada geese, white-fronted geese,

MARSH WORLD by ANGUS SHORTT
Ducks Unlimited

GREEN-WINGED TEAL (Anas carolinense)

Smallest of the dabblers, the breeding range of this trim little duck extends from the Maritimes across Canada and from the central U.S. to Alaska. It is an early spring migrant, arriving soon after first pintail and mallard and well ahead of the blue-winged teal. Nests are located on dry land, usually well concealed in a grass clump or beneath low shrubs. Southward migration is leisurely the birds lingering as long as marshes with good feeding spots remain unfrozen.

68 - '71

This is one of the 112 "Marsh World" series I produced for Ducks Unlimited in the late 1960s and early 1970s. Each had a small illustration and a few words about an aspect of aquatic flora or fauna. They were reproduced in newspapers and sporting and wildlife magazines.

snow geese and brant. Backgrounds varied: marshes for most ducks, grain fields for mallard and Canada geese. Brant and white-fronted geese had a west coast mountain setting. As well I painted a number of ducks and geese on water, a pair of mallards standing among reeds and a pintail pair in snow by the edge of a spring pond.

After I retired from Ducks Unlimited, in 1973, I put aside my paints and brushes until the spring of 1974. Then, while going through my files of field sketches, I felt the urge to paint some of our native sparrows, which had always appealed to me, including the white-crowned, white-throated, Harris's and fox. I did them in watercolor, the backgrounds a simple cluster of leaves in fall colors, or a spray of jackpine or spruce, taken from the many pencil drawings I had made and filed away for future use.

Along with the sparrows, I did a series of owls in similar settings. At the opening of a retrospective exhibition of my paintings at the new, expanded Manitoba Museum of Man and Nature in 1975, I noticed a change

Great Gray Owl
1970
watercolor on mat board
19 $^{13}/_{16}$" x 15 $^{15}/_{16}$"
Collection of George Cotter, Winnipeg

I have always been interested in owls because of their silent flight and nocturnal habits.

Pelicans
1966
oil on masonite
19" x 47 $\frac{1}{4}$"
Collection of George Cotter, Winnipeg

George Cotter and I canoed to an island on Dog Lake, which is just east of the center of Lake Manitoba, where pelicans were nesting. I sketched the pelicans and cormorants and their young from the canoe. They nest on the island because neither species has any way to defend its young.

Mallards on the Move
1977
oil on canvas board
30" x 22"
Collection of Ducks Unlimited, Memphis

This was painted for the cover of the September/October issue of Ducks Unlimited magazine. It was painted to commemorate Ducks Unlimited Canada's fortieth birthday. It features a view of Big Grass Marsh, the first donor project, seen from a bird's-eye view.

Autumn's Bounty
1977
oil on canvas board
22" x 30"
Collection of Ducks Unlimited, Memphis

This was the second version of a view of Big Grass Marsh that I painted for the fortieth anniversary of the founding of Ducks Unlimited Canada. I painted it from a human's-eye view. Prints of the painting were sold to interested collectors across North America. It was a very successful fund-raiser.

Our son, Terry, took this photograph of Betsy and me on our fiftieth wedding anniversary in 1989.

in public taste. Ladies in particular were either fascinated or repelled by the owls. I have a feeling this was because of the expression in the birds' eyes.

Not only were predatory birds more fashionable, the public was becoming sympathetic to the conservation of wetlands. In 1977, in honor of its fortieth anniversary the next year, Ducks Unlimited commissioned me to paint a 20" x 24" oil depicting its first project, the restoration of the Big Grass Marsh. I made a full-size pencil drawing in detail. It showed the concrete control dam, the marsh, flocks of mallards coming in and, in the background, a dragline building nesting islands. This was a horizontal format. Betsy looked it over and liked it, but suggested I do another in a vertical layout. Her intuition about my paintings has never been at fault, so I set to work and drew a second one. This had the same features as the first, except that the marsh was viewed from the air. High above the marsh, I painted a pair of mallards, fairly large and detailed, and below them a flock of six winging in, with other flocks in the distance.

Ducks Unlimited liked the drawings so much I was commissioned to paint them both. The horizontal version was reproduced as full-size prints to be sold to new members for $25; the vertical design, in an oval format bordered with silver, was reproduced on the cover of the anniversary issue of the Ducks Unlimited magazine.

Ducks Unlimited, in partnership with the Manitoba government, was now working on an ambitious, controversial restoration project, the Oak Hammock Marsh, fifteen miles northwest of Winnipeg. The role of Ducks Unlimited in wetland conservation caught the attention of a film producer, John Leckie, and in 1979, I was featured in Leckie's half-hour documentary "Wings to the Future," broadcast on the CBC television program *This Land*. I was interviewed and filmed painting both in my garret studio and in a red canoe at Oak Hammock Marsh.

The 1980s were among my most productive years. Many paintings were commissioned, and I had the opportunity to portray a variety of bird species. In addition to ducks, I painted bald eagles, songbirds, and a Kirtland's warbler, a very rare bird that, in the north, is found only in north-central Michigan.

Throughout the 1990s my desire to paint continued, although I stopped accepting commissions. Betsy and I also continued our birding expeditions. Oak Hammock Marsh was one of my favorite destinations. Although I was usually more interested in the hawks and shorebirds than I was in the waterfowl, when the marsh's interpretation center opened in 1993, I donated a new oil painting showing snow geese in the marsh with the building in the distance. My last large oil painting, done in 1996, depicted Canada and snow geese in the same setting and was my personal commitment to the future of Oak Hammock Marsh as a center for research and education.

Canada and Snow Geese at Oak Hammock Marsh
1996
oil on canvas board
23" x 29"
Collection of Lindsay Lanphear, Winnipeg

I painted this for a Ducks Unlimited fundraising auction. It includes two species of geese that always fly through Oak Hammock Marsh. The building in the distance is the Ducks Unlimited Canada Oak Hammock Marsh Conservation Centre, 20 miles north of Winnipeg.

Afterword: Ducks Unlimited's Freshwater Initiative

When Ducks Unlimited was founded in 1937 by sportsmen, its focus was on preserving wetlands for the wildlife, especially ducks, that inhabited these areas. Bill Leitch, DU's first chief biologist, observed, "The assumption was that more water would equal more ducks, so DU essentially became an engineering organization, building dikes and dams to store water."

In the early years, abundant tracts of native prairie remained, and when the water supplies were restored, the ducks thrived. But the landscapes used by ducks did not remain untouched. By the 1970s Ducks Unlimited realized that its simple approach to restoring and protecting wetlands was no longer enough. The landscapes that had supported prairie ducks were also losing the uplands, which are critical nesting areas.

In the 1980s, the organization began to approach conservation with an eye to restoring and protecting all the critical elements of the landscapes used by waterfowl. The other plants and wildlife that shared these landscapes also benefited from this attention, as did humans.

Throughout the years, water remained at the center of Ducks Unlimited's work, although lately, in addition to the concerns about wildlife, there is a growing recognition of the importance of wetlands as a source of clean, clear water for human needs as well. As Brad Jones wrote in Ducks Unlimited Canada *Conservator*, the wetlands act as "huge ecological sponges by soaking up pollutants and filtering water before it reaches your tap."

Recognizing that problems with water continue to threaten the quality of life for people and wildlife in North America, and throughout the world, in recent years Ducks Unlimited has strengthened its commitment to learning more about the issues affecting water in today's world through its Fresh Water Initiative. The initiative focuses on matters as far-reaching as groundwater replenishment, flood control, nutrient and contaminant management and climate change — all critical factors for the conservation of fresh water. Because of the support that has been provided by private citizens for more than sixty years, Ducks Unlimited has the experience, capabilities and commitment to put this new information to work as soon as it is available.

Angus Shortt was a leader in helping the organization grow into the key position it now holds. In recognition of the enduring strength of Angus Shortt's art and his contribution to Ducks Unlimited, the publisher has donated the costs and proceeds from the sale of this book to Ducks Unlimited's Freshwater Initiative.

Mallards Coming into a Marsh After Rain
1962
oil on canvas board
21 ⁷/₈″ x 27 ¹⁵/₁₆″
Collection of Richard Bonnycastle, Calgary

For my paintings, I first traced the birds in position on a dry background. Then I painted the body and upper wing, then the head, neck and the shadow on the body. Next I did the lower wing. The fine details were done last, after the rest was dry.

Biographical Notes

Education

1926	Linwood High School, St. James. Grade ten.
1928–1929	Winnipeg School of Art (part of Brigden's Graphic Arts training program).

Professional Experience

1926-1931	Wood Engraver, Printer, Brigden's, Winnipeg.
1935–1938	Artist/Technician, Manitoba Museum, Winnipeg.
1938	Artist/Taxidermist, American Museum of Natural History, New York.
1937–1938	Surveyor of bird populations in western Manitoba, National Museum of Canada, Ottawa.
1939–1973, 1977–1986	Artist (multi-media), Ducks Unlimited Canada, Winnipeg.
1945–1960	Photographer and Botanical Artist, T & T Seeds, Winnipeg.
c. 1945	Artist, *Hawks of Western Canada*, Ducks Unlimited, Winnipeg. With Bert Cartwright.
1945	Artist, *Know Your Ducks and Geese* monograph, *Sports Afield* magazine, Minneapolis.
1948	Artist, *Co-operation Unlimited*, Ducks Unlimited Canada, Winnipeg. With Ed Russenholt.
1949	Illustrator, *Ducks Are Different* book, published by Provost News, Alberta. With Frank Holmes.
1949	Artist, *Birds of Prey* issue, Sports Afield magazine, Minneapolis, Minnesota.
1951	Artist, *North American Hawks & Eagles* issue, *Sports Afield* magazine, Minneapolis.
1952	Artist, *Owls* issue, *Sports Afield* magazine, Minneapolis.
1962	Commissioned Designer of Confederation medallions, K. Bileski Stamp Dealer, Winnipeg.
1963	Commissioned Designer of 15-cent Canada Geese stamp, Post Office Department, Ottawa.
1963– c. 1970	Commissioned Artist, K. Bileski Stamp Dealer, Winnipeg.
1964	Writer/Illustrator, "Wild Wings" weekly column, *Winnipeg Tribune*.
1971–1975	Illustrator, *Marsh World* book, Ducks Unlimited Canada, Winnipeg.
1977	Commissioned Artist, 40th Anniversary of Ducks Unlimited Canada, Chicago, cover design for Ducks Unlimited magazine, September/October issue.
1977	Commissioned Designer, United States Playing Card Co., Cincinnati.
1990	Plaque Designer for Alf Hole Wildlife Sanctuary, Ducks Unlimited Canada, Winnipeg.

Selected Volunteer Experience

1933–1940s	Lecturer, Artist, Photographer, Natural History Society of Manitoba, Winnipeg.
1934	Surveyor of bird populations in Lake St. Martin area, Royal Ontario Museum, Toronto.
1945–1963	Lecturer/Photographer, Winnipeg Horticultural Society.
1947–1949	President, Natural History Society of Manitoba, Winnipeg.
1965–1974	Honorary President, Manitoba Naturalist's Society, Winnipeg.

Prairie Elevators with Geese
1984
oil on canvas board
14" x 18"
Collection of Jim and Ann May, Winnipeg

I did a series of paintings with flocks of birds landing in swathed grain fields. I sometimes put elevators in the scenes. Now, of course, they have all but disappeared.

Selected Exhibitions

1929–62	**Annual Exhibition (with Betsy Shortt's flower displays)**, Natural History Society of Manitoba, Winnipeg
1932	**Bird Art Exhibit,** American Ornithologists' Union, St. Louis, Missouri.
1932	**Nature art display by Natural History Society of Manitoba**, T. Eaton Co. Annex, Winnipeg.
1942–1986	**Exhibits for fund-raising events**, Ducks Unlimited, various sites across the United States.
1945	**Solo exhibit**, Ducks Unlimited U.S. meeting, Fort Garry Hotel, Winnipeg.
1946	**Group exhibit**, Society for the Prevention of Cruelty to Animals, Johannesburg.
c. 1950 –1970	**Group exhibitions**, Zesbaugh Gallery, Minneapolis, Minnesota.
c. 1950 –1970	**Group exhibitions**, Loch Mayberry Gallery, Winnipeg.
1958	**Nature art exhibit**, American Ornithologists' Union annual meeting, Saskatchewan Museum of Natural History, Regina.
1972	**Nature art exhibit**, American Ornithologists' Union annual meeting, Convention Center. Grand Forks, North Dakota.
1975	**Animals in Art Exhibition**, Royal Ontario Museum, Toronto. Sponsored by World Wildlife Fund.
1999	**Solo display**, Youville Centre, Winnipeg.

Collections

L. Barkhausen, Chicago
H. Birr, San Francisco
A. Cooper, Baton Rouge, Louisiana
G. Cotter, Winnipeg
Ducks Unlimited
A. Glassell, Shreeveport, Louisiana
F. Hingst, Clio, Michigan
J. Moermond, Midland, Michigan
J. Morton, Winnipeg
Richardson Family, Winnipeg
J. Robinson, Minneapolis
O. Sprungman, San Diego
Private collections in all provinces of Canada, in each of the United States and in Japan, South Africa, Sweden, Ireland, England and Australia

Awards

1939	**Shortt Lake,** 75 miles east southeast of Fort McMurray, Alberta, named by Ducks Unlimited for Angus
1946	**Bronze Medal** for original research and artistic merit in ornithology, Natural History Society of Manitoba, Winnipeg.
1947	**Elected Member**, American Ornithologists' Union, St. Louis, Missouri.
1969	**Good Citizenship Award**, Manitoba Travel and Convention Bureau, Winnipeg.
1970	**Centennial Gold Medal of Remembrance,** Manitoba Historical Society, Winnipeg.
1974	**Honorary Life Membership**, Manitoba Naturalists Society, Winnipeg.
1981	**Art Award** for contributions to preservation of North America's Wildlife Heritage, Ducks Unlimited Canada, Winnipeg.
1987	**Ralph D. Bird Award**, Manitoba Naturalists Society, Winnipeg.
2001	**Angus Shortt Habitat Project**, 10 miles south of Oak Lake, Manitoba, named by Ducks Unlimited
2003	**Queen's Golden Jubilee Medal**

Black-bellied Whistling Ducks
March 1989
Oil on canvas board
16" x 20"
Collection of Mrs. Jean Moermond, Midland, Minnesota

These ducks are found as far north as the southern part of Texas and as far south as west-central Mexico. This painting, done for the late Jack Moremond, an avid collector who became a friend, shows them in a mangrove swamp. One is in juvenile plumage.

Goshawk and Gray Partridge
1949
oil on canvas board
20" x 15 $^7/_8$"
Collection of the artist

I painted this for an article Bert Cartwright was preparing for Sports Afield *magazine. The winter scene shows two goshawks, one mature and the other immature, hunting gray partridge, once known as Hungarian partridge. The magazine didn't use the painting because they felt their readership wouldn't be interested in reading about birds that hunters normally shot and discarded as worthless.*

Misty Morning – Canada Geese
March 1987
oil on canvas board
18" x 24"
Collection of the artist

This type of painting was very popular with collectors. I painted the geese coming in from either the left or the right. Quite often I would have a request to paint the collector's favorite hunting spot in a field, along with specific types of birds.

Blackburnian Warbler
1974
watercolor on mat board
12 $^1/_{16}$" x 10 $^1/_8$"
Collection of the artist

When we went out one day, Betsy found a small, delicate branch with two open dead pinecones covered with lichen. We brought it home, and I used it as a perch for this bird study.

Illustration Identification

These small illustrations appear at the beginning of each chapter:

Chapter One: page 11
An ink drawing of a canvasback pair on the water.

Chapter Two: page 16
A wood engraving of a jackknife – one of many I made for the Eaton's catalog as part of my work at Brigden's.

Chapter Three: page 19
An ink drawing of a pair of redheads.

Chapter Four, page 25
A pair of blue-winged teals submitted as a design for a Migratory Bird Hunting Stamp in the 1940s. These hunting permit stamps were sold to licensed hunters, with the proceeds going to a conservation fund to help to maintain waterfowl life in the United States.

Chapter Five: page 35
One of four drawings of the heads of big game animals I did for place cards at the Ducks Unlimited annual dinner in Calgary in 1945.

Chapter Six, page 43
A 1945 pencil sketch of a hovering rough-legged hawk in its black phase.

Chapter Seven: page 53
A great horned owl done on scratchboard.

Chapter Eight: page 65
An ink drawing of two peregrine falcons done in 1949. The top bird is an adult, the bottom, immature.

Index

Note: Page numbers in italics indicate an illustration.

A
albatross, wandering, 51
American Museum of Natural History, 23, 50
Atkinson, George, 36
Audubon, John James, 22
Autumn's Bounty, 81

B
Bajkov, Alexander, 54–55, *55*
Bald Eagle and Osprey, 73
Belted Kingfisher (Female), 49
Big Grass Marsh, restoration project, 53–54, 82
"The Big Marsh Lives Again" (movie), 75
    bird surveys
    Dauphin area, 50
    Lake St. Martin, 35–36
    northwestern Manitoba, 43–48
    Saskeram marshes, 54
The Birds of Canada (Taverner), 19
"Birds of New York State" (Fuertes), 26
Birds of Western Canada (Taverner), 19, 23, 26
bittern, 26
Black-bellied Whistling Ducks, 89
blackbirds, 28
red-winged, 26, 55
Blackburnian Warbler, 92
Blue Jay, 17
bluebills. See scaups, lesser
Bluebills, Lake Francis Marsh, Manitoba, 62
bobolink, 26
brant, 76
Brooks, Allan, 22–23

C
Canada and Snow Geese at Oak Hammock Marsh, 83
Canvasbacks, Delta, Manitoba, 10
Canvasbacks in Stormy Weather, 69
Canvasbacks, Netley Marshes, Lake Winnipeg, 68

Cartwright, Bert, 22, 33, 36, 37, 51, 54, 61, 75
    "Wild Wings" column, 19
CBC television, 82
chickadees, 28, 31, 42, 61
cormorants, 31
Cotter, George, 75, 79
cranes, sandhill, 54, 59
crows, 26

D
dowitchers, 47
Duckological report, 58
ducks, 47, 82. *See also* mallards
    black, 76
    black-bellied whistling, 89
    canvasback, 10, 11, 47, 61, 65, 68, 69, 76, 93
    crow, 31
    fish. *see* mergansers
    harlequin, 24
    pintail, 40, 52, 54, 61, 65
    Northern, 76
    redhead, 19, 93
Ducks and Men (Leitch), 58
Ducks Unlimited Canada, 51, 53–64
    big game animals place cards, 35, 93
    Big Grass Marsh, 75
    brochure, 75–76
    Christmas card, 22, 93
    Fresh Water Initiative, 84
Ducks Unlimited Canada *Conservator*, 84

E
"The Eagle Through the Ages," *37*
eagles, 37
    bald, 73, 82
    golden, 41
Edge of the Poplar Bluff, 14
eider, king, 66

F
Fanset, George, 54
15-cent Canada geese stamp, 74
finches, purple, 45, 51
Fisher, W.C., 61
flycatchers

alder, 47
least, 45
olive-sided, 45
Fuertes, Louis Agassiz, 22–23, 26

G
Game Birds and Animals in Manitoba, 75
geese, 87
    blue, 38, 54
    Canada, 54, 65, 74–75, 76, 83, 91
    stamp, 74
    lesser snow, 38
    Ross', 72
    snow, 38, 54, 76, 82, 83
    white-fronted, 76
The Gladstone Age Press, 53
goshawk, 90
Goshawk and Gray Partridge, 90
Grant's Lake, 38–39
Gray Partridge in Snow, 64
Great Gray Owl, 77
grebes, eared, 47
grosbeaks, 28, 61
grouse
    pinnated, 41
    ruffed, 26, 28, 34, 51
    sharp-tailed, 12, 28
gulls, Franklin's, 39

H
Haak, Adrian, 38
Haak, Betsy. See Shortt, Betsy (Mrs. Angus)
Hall, Joseph, 16
Harlequin Ducks, 24
Hatch, David, 74
Hatton, Horace, 30
hawks
    broad-winged, 26
    Cooper's, 26
    marsh, 54
    nighthawks, 45
    red-tailed, 30, 33
    rough-legged, 43, 93
    sharp-shinned, 45
    sparrow, 31
Head and Foot of Osprey (Adult Male), 32

Heard, Jack, 55
heron, 26
Hooded Mergansers, 4
hummingbirds, ruby-throated, 26, 31, 36, 38

J
jackknife (wood engraving), 15, 93
Jaques, Francis Lee, 23, 51
jays
    blue, 17, 22, 28, 31, 61
    Canada, 22
Jessiman, Duncan, 64
Jones, Brad, 84
Juvenile Black-capped Chickadee, 42

K
killdeers, 26
King Eider, 66
kingbirds, 26
kingfishers, 26
Knight, Charles R., 51
Know Your Ducks and Geese, 61

L
Lake St. Martin, 36
    bird survey, 35–36
"The Lake That Waits" (prospectus), 60
larks, horned, 26, 30
Lawrence, Alex, 36
Leckie, John, 82
Leitch, W.G. (Bill), 52, 58, 84
LeMoine FitzGerald, L., 15–16, 23
longspurs
    chestnut-collared, 26
Loons at Dawn, 63

M
Main, Tom, 54, 58, 60–61, 65
Mallard Pair, 18
mallards, 18, 47, 54, 61, 65, 76. *See also*
    ducks
Mallards Coming Into a Marsh After Rain, 85
Mallards on the Move, 80
Mallards over a Stooked Grain Field,
    Manitoba, 67
Manitoba

habitat, 35–36
    map, 8
Manitoba Museum of Man and Nature, 76
"Marsh World" series, 76
meadowlarks, 26
    western, 27
    mergansers, 2, 4
Migratory Bird Act (Canada), 38
Migratory Bird Hunting Stamp, 25, 93
Misty Morning - Canada Geese, 91
Moremond, Jack, 89
Morton, Jim, 59

N
Natural History Society of Manitoba, 31, 33
    museum, 36, 48

O
Oak Hammock Marsh, 82
Orioles, 70
orioles, Baltimore, 31
ospreys, 32, 73
owls, 29–30, 76, 82
    boreal, 29, 29
    great gray, 77
    great horned, 53, 93
    horned, 26
    long-eared, 31
    Richardson's, 28
    saw-whet, 29
    snowy, 21, 30

P
partridges, gray, 31, 64, 90
Pelicans, 78-79
peregrine falcons, 65, 93
Peterson Field Guides, 23
Peterson, Roger Tory, 23
pewees, wood, 26
Pintails (1949), 52
Pintails (1968), 40
pipit, Sprague's, 26, 46, 47
Potter, John, 51
prairie chicken. *See* grouse, pinnated
Prairie Elevators with Geese, 87

R
rails, 55
    sora, 26
    Virginia, 48
    yellow, 44–45, 47
redheads, 19, 93
Richardson Brothers art store, 31
Riding Mountain National Park, 50
Ross' Geese, 72
Royal Ontario Museum (Ontario), 23, 35–36
Ruddy Turnstone, 60
Ruffed Grouse in Poplar Woods, 34
Russenholt, Ed, 54, 58, 60

S
Sandhill Cranes, 59
scaups, 76
    lesser, 47, 62
scoters
    common, 56, 57
    surf, 56, 57
    white-winged, 56, 57
Sharp-tailed Grouse Dancing, 12
Shortt, Angus
    at Brigden's, 15–18
    early years, 11–18
    and the Great Depression, 25–34
    health of, 55, 58
    honors and awards, 75
    and marriage of, 50, 54
    painting techniques, 65, 68
    photographs of, *28, 33, 39, 45, 48, 50, 58,*
        61, 82
    works
        Autumn's Bounty, 81
        Bald Eagle and Osprey, 73
        Belted Kingfisher (Female), 49
        Black-bellied Whistling Ducks, 89
        Blackburnian Warbler, 92
        Blue Jay, 17
        Bluebills, Lake Francis Marsh,
            Manitoba, 62
        Canada and Snow Geese at Oak
            Hammock Marsh, 83
        Canvasbacks, Delta, Manitoba, 10
        Canvasbacks in Stormy Weather, 69

Canvasbacks, Netley Marshes, Lake Winnipeg, 68
Edge of the Poplar Bluff, 14
15-cent Canada geese stamp, 74
Goshawk and Gray Partridge, 90
Gray Partridge in Snow, 64
Great Gray Owl, 77
Harlequin Ducks, 24
Head and Foot of Osprey (Adult Male), 32
Hooded Mergansers, 4
Juvenile Black-capped Chickadee, 42
King Eider, 66
Loons at Dawn, 63
Mallard Pair, 18
Mallards Coming Into a Marsh After Rain, 85
Mallards on the Move, 80
Mallards over a Stooked Grain Field, Manitoba, 67
Misty Morning - Canada Geese, 91
Orioles, 70
Pelicans, 78-79
Pintails (1949), 52
Pintails (1968), 40
Prairie Elevators with Geese, 87
Ross' Geese, 72
Ruddy Turnstone, 60
Ruffed Grouse in Poplar Woods, 34
Sandhill Cranes, 59
Sharp-tailed Grouse Dancing, 12
Sketch for Hooded Merganser, 2
Snowy Owl Near Rosser, Manitoba, 21
Sprague's Pipit (Immature), 46
Tundra Swans at Sunrise, 71
Western Meadowlark: Adult and Young, 27
White-winged, Surf and Common Scoters (oil on canvas board), 57
White-winged, Surf and Common Scoters (sketch), 56
Shortt, Betsy (Mrs. Angus), 33, 33, 33, 50, 54, 82
Shortt, Emma McMeekin (mother), 11–12
Shortt, Henry (father), 11
Shortt, Michael (uncle), 11
Shortt, Terry (brother), 11–13, 19, 23

Shortt, Terry (son), 65
shovelers, 47, 54
    Northern, 47
Silver Heights farm. *See* Strathcona Estate
Sketch for Hooded Merganser, 2
snipes, Wilson's, 45
Snowy Owl Near Rosser, Manitoba, 21
Soper, J. Dewey, 38, 44
South Pacific petrels, 51
sparrows, 28, 76
    clay-colored, 33, 47
    fox, 76
    Harris's, 76
    house, 28
    Nelson's, 45
    savannah, 26
    sharp-tailed, 45
    swamp, 48
    white-crowned, 76
    white-throated, 76
Sports Afield magazine, 61
Sprague's Pipit (Immature), 46
Stevens, D.M., 53–54
Strathcona Estate, 12–13, 19
    habitats, 26
Sutton, Richard, 50
    swallows
    bank, 26
    rough-winged, 26
swans
    tundra, 71
    whistling, 31

T
Taverner, Percy A., 19, 22–23
    northwestern Manitoba bird survey, 43–48
    and red-tailed hawk skins, 30–31
    on work of Shortt brothers, 20, 22
taxidermy, 30, 51
teals
    blue-winged, 25, 54, 76, 93
    green-winged, 65, 76, 76
terns
    black, 47
    Forster's, 47
Tundra Swans at Sunrise, 71

V
vultures, 51

W
Waller, Sam, 35–36
    cottage of, 36
warblers, 28
    Blackburnian, 92
    Canada, 45
    chestnut-sided, 45
    Connecticut, 47
    Kirtland's, 82
    magnolia, 45
    mourning, 45
    Tennessee, 45
    yellow-throated, 26
Watkins, Bill, 38–39, 43–48, 45
waxwings
    bohemian, 28
    cedar, 26, 45
Western Meadowlark: Adult and Young, 27
White-winged, Surf and Common Scoters (oil on canvas board), 57
White-winged, Surf and Common Scoters (sketch), 56
Whitman, Reg, 31
wigeon, 47, 54, 61, 76
    American, 47
wildflowers, 28
Wildlife Conservation Digest, 75
Wildlife Crusader, 75
"Wings to the Future" (CBC television), 82
Winnipeg School of Art, 15, 23
Winnipeg Tribune, "Wild Wings" column, 19, 37, 75
wrens
    house, 45
    short-billed marsh, 26

Y
yellowlegs, greater, 45
yellowthroats, Northern, 47